FOREST TOWN
The Village That Grew out of Coal

The Development of a Twentieth Century Nottinghamshire Village

Pauline Marples

Published by
Forest Town Heritage Group
2005

Other Books relating to Forest Town

The Forest Town Hostel 1944 - 1959
by Pauline & Malcolm Marples
ISBN 1-904 102-20-4

Web Sites relating to Forest Town
www.foresttowncrier.org.uk
www.mp-marples.co.uk
www.forest-town.info

Published by Forest Town Heritage Group.

Printed by
Reliance Advertising and Business Printers,
Stanton Mill, Bath Lane, Mansfield NG18 2BZ

ISBN 0-9551446-0-4
ISBN 978-0-9551446-0-8

The publication of this book has been assisted by a grant from the Nottinghamshire Community Foundation.

CONTENTS

PAGE

Contents ... iii
Abbreviations ... iii
Illustrations ... iv
Acknowledgements ... vi
Notes ... vi
Preface ... vii

1 Introduction ... 1
2 Looking Back ... 5
3 Land Owner and Colliery Company ... 9
4 The 'Ground Rules' (the Colliery and Conservation) ... 11
5 The Farms ... 13
6 Planning the Colliery and the Village ... 19
7 Sinking and the Discovery of Coal ... 23
8 The Avenues ... 27
9 St David's Mission, the First Anglican Church ... 33
10 St Alban's Church ... 39
11 The Methodists ... 47
12 The Village School ... 57
13 The Village Shops ... 67
14 The Institute ... 75
15 The Drill Hall ... 89
16 The Singing Miner ... 97
17 Forest Town and Royalty ... 103
18 The War Years ... 111
19 People and Events ... 125
20 The Expanding Village ... 135

Bibliography 141
General Index 143
Place Index 147
Name Index 148

ABBREVIATIONS

BCC	Bolsover Colliery Company
BPMA	British Postal Museum and Archives
DRO	Derbyshire Record Office
NA	Nottinghamshire Archives
NUHL	Nottingham University Hallward Library
PRO	Public Record Office (now National Archive Office)

ILLUSTRATIONS

A disappearing hedge 17th March 2000 ... 1
The first houses ... 2
The ruins of King John's Palace ... 5
Crown Farm ... 13
James Newton with horse ... 14
Evidence of outbuildings at the Travellers Rest 1994 ... 15
The Travellers Rest circa 1910 ... 16
An early photograph of graves in St Alban's Churchyard ... 22
The Sinkers circ 1904/5. ... 24
Wire Gauge belonging to enginewright Tom Wakefield. ... 25
Mansfield Colliery. ... 26
The Avenue Houses. ... 29
Tin Bath and Outside Toilet. ... 30
The Avenues circa 1907 & 1908. ... 31
In front of 23 Fourth Avenue. ... 32
St David's Mission Church. ... 34
Margaret Bull. ... 35
Forest Town Mission FC 1909. ... 35
Book 'The Brown Bird.' ... 36
Foundation Stone St Alban's Church. ... 39
Stone Laying Ceremony 1910. ... 41
Consecration Pamphlet 1911. ... 43
St Alban's Church. ... 44
Church organ. ... 46
Foundation Stones ... 48
Methodist Church ... 49
Joseph Share. ... 50
Drill Hall. ... 53
Wesleyan Chapel. ... 54
Miss Stafford and Children. ... 60
Mr Rudge and Children. ... 62
Certificate of Merit. ... 63
School Book. ... 63
In the Classroom 1913. ... 65
Infants Class 1916. ... 65
Bertha Buxton. ... 68
The Co-op. ... 69
Forest View. ... 69
Forest Town Stores etc. ... 72
Shops. ... 73
Plans Workman's Institute. ... 76
The Forest Town Miners' Institute. ... 77
Tennis Courts. ... 80
Colliery Sport ... 80
Colliery Band - Jack Cupit ... 82
Colliery Band - Harry Roulston ... 83

Mr & Mrs Daxon. 83
Pit Ponies. 85
Peace Memento. 86
Opening of Drill Hall. 91
Boys' Brigade Badge. 92
Drill Hall. 94
Patrons & Committee Joint Winners Earl Haigh Cup 1922. 95
Concert Poster 1906. 97
Morgan Kingston. 98
Concert Poster Metropolitan Opera House. 99
Programme Royal Visit 1914. 104
Elijah & Sarah Mottishaw. 106
Royal Visitors leaving No 8 Second Avenue 1914 107
Officials being presented - Royal Visit 1914. 108
Souvenir Medals. 109
On the corner of First Avenue. 111
Boys' Brigade. 111
Entrance to the Drill Hall. 112
Clipstone Camp. 115
Marching Soldiers. 115
Soldiers on Walkers Plantation. 117
Montague Osler - Taxi. 119
Military Funeral. 120
Unveiling of Roll of Honour. 121
War Memorial. 122
Marquee and Swings. 126
Mansfield Colliery Cricket Club 1919. 130
Envelope to Miss P Daxon. 131
Wedding of Sydney Bacon to Phyllis M Daxon. 132
George Street. 135
Old Mill Lane. 136
The expanding village 139

ACKNOWLEDGEMENTS

First and foremost to the people of Forest Town for their support, encouragement and interest over the past thirteen years. There are too many people to name individually and sadly some of them have not lived long enough to read my book.

To tutors and colleagues at Nottingham University, for if I had not embarked on the Certificate in Local History, my interest in Forest Town would never have materialised.

To staff of many Libraries and Local Studies Libraries including Forest Town, Mansfield Woodhouse, Mansfield, Sutton-in-Ashfield, Nottingham, Chesterfield, and the Hallward Library, Nottingham University. The staff of Record/Archive Offices at Nottingham, Matlock (Derbyshire) and the National Archives London. The curator, and staff at Mansfield Museum and Art Gallery. Morgan Kingston researchers and genealogists. The Evening Post archivist, The Old Mansfield Society archivist, and Mr Linney.

To friends and colleagues both past and present at St Alban's Church and the Trinity Methodist Church, including the late Rev G Fawcett.

To past and present staff of Forest Town School who helped with records and other information.

To everyone who has helped with documents and photographs.

To my good friend Shirley for proof reading the manuscript, also Nigel and Tony of Reliance Printers for advice on layout and production.

To my family and friends who have now learned to 'live with Forest Town', especially my husband Malcolm who is now as much a part of it all as I am.

If anyone has been inadvertently missed please accept my apologies, everyone's help has been appreciated.

NOTES

While every attempt has been made to give the correct spelling of peoples names, they have been found to vary in different records and newspaper reports. Anything that could not be clearly read has been underlined e.g. page 55, *C. O. <u>Oivers.</u>* Where oral history has been used, it has to be accepted these are peoples memories, however in most cases the same story will have been heard from various people.

Attempts have been made to contact copyright owners where appropriate. If any have been inadvertently missed out this will be rectified in future editions.

PREFACE

With the demise of the coalmines it is important to remember why and how their communities were established, and this book attempts to do just that. No known work has previously been published on Forest Town, and it is appropriate that this initial history is published in 2005 when the village is celebrating one hundred years since the discovery of coal at Mansfield Colliery, the building of the first Anglican church, and the first Methodist church. *See Forest Town 2005 Celebrations (www.forest-town.info)*

The book looks at the first 21 years from around 1900 and gives an insight into specific establishments, people and events during those early years. Each chapter stands up in its own right and can be read individually, or to discover the wider picture of this interesting community the book should be read as a whole.

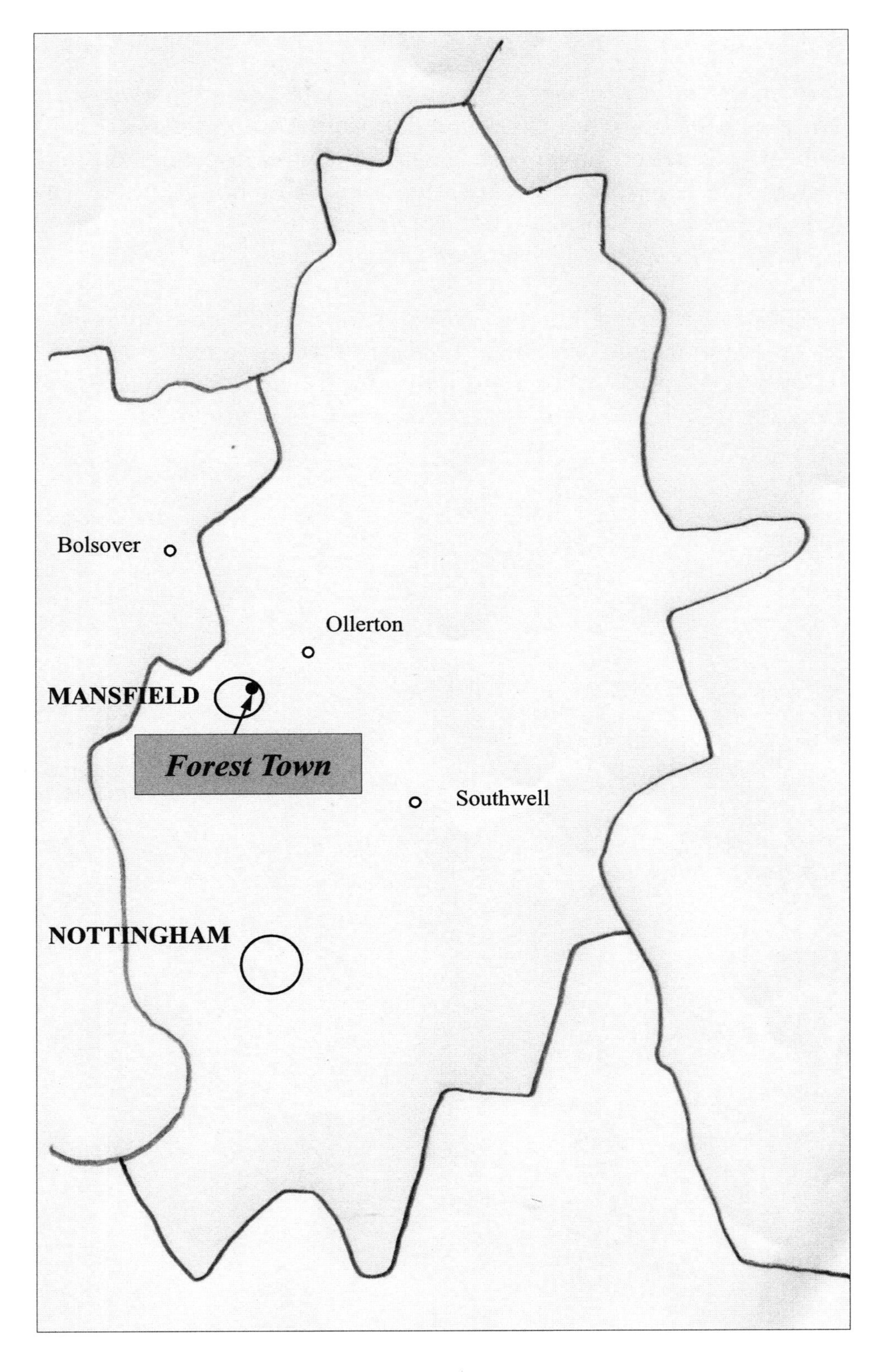

The County of Nottinghamshire
showing Forest Town

1 - INTRODUCTION

Forest Town at the beginning of the twenty-first century, is a large sprawling village which has now become an expansion of Mansfield, a market town in Nottinghamshire. The village is within close proximity to the Derbyshire border.

The local people still recall when Forest Town was just a small mining community, surrounded by fields and heath land, with areas where people could walk freely and children play safely. Today many of the fields and hedges have disappeared. They have been replaced with tarmac roads and brick buildings of every size, colour and description. It has grown into an area of residential housing that is continuing to expand into the few surrounding areas of countryside that remain. This long term growth of new housing estates is called 'progress'!

For many years, various planning authorities have decided what people in the local community need to enhance their lives: schools, shops, health centres, libraries and leisure facilities. All of the decisions have resulted in the noise and vibration of earth moving machines becoming a part of every day life.

The machines move round in the name of progress and they ruthlessly move trees, earth, and rock. In doing so they destroy the last vestiges of the local heritage, and they speedily change the face of the landscape forever.[1]

'A disappearing hedge' on Elmhurst Road, 17th March 2000. The hedge, being ripped up in preparation of a new road and housing estate

In 1900, the scenario was very different and yet it had many similarities to the present day.[2] The local landscape was a wide area of open land, green fields and trees. It was a landscape that over the past century has gradually been transformed out of all recognition because people have moved into the area to live and to work. People who needed houses, schools, shops and other essential facilities. They were all part of a new development, a development in the first decades of the twentieth century was also termed as 'progress.'

Once a field, these were the first houses to be built in Forest Town between 1903 -1909
They were named The Avenues

At the root of those early changes was the pioneering enterprise of our predecessors, the desire of men to work, and the nation's demand for coal. These three ingredients; enterprise, work, and coal, were the foundations of the new village, and the community spirit of Forest Town. A community that evolved round the sinking of a new coal mine, Mansfield Colliery or 'Crown Farm Pit (Crownie)' as it became known locally to most people.

The Bolsover Colliery Company from Derbyshire sank this new coal mine, and in doing so provided work for hundreds of men for the best part of a century. It added to the income of the colliery owners, also the local landowner, the Duke of Portland as royalties were paid to the Duke on coal output. Mansfield Colliery became well known for its coal production, and at one time was the largest coal producing coal mine in the country.[3]

The early development of this colliery and the building of the associated village of Forest Town, are part of both national and local history. They have a history to be proud of, it is a history that deserves to be told, and a history which should be preserved for future generations.

This book covers the foundation years of Forest Town by introducing the initial development of the colliery and the growth of the village. In those early years, (roughly up to 1921), readers will not find a chapter on the Catholic Church, or the village pub; it was many years before these were established in the village. While early documentation regarding drinking establishments i.e. the Institute has been found, no mention has to date been discovered of anyone of the Catholic faith during those early years.

NOTES

1 In the spring of 1998 the fields between Old Mill Lane and New Mill Lane were reshaped, vast amounts of rock was destroyed to make way for a new road, supermarket etc. On 13th March 2000 earth moving machines moved onto fields between Elmhurst Road and Heatherley Drive, the roads and hedges which had been there for many years were ripped up. The author has watched all this from her home.
2 This book which has been researched over a number of years is being written in 2000/2005.
3 Bolsover Jubilee Souvenir 1889 – 1939.

2 - LOOKING BACK

Forest Town is situated on the road from Ollerton to Mansfield. It is a tarmac road, busy with noisy fast moving traffic, cars, lorries, buses, and other vehicles of every size and description. Everywhere there are buildings, houses, shops, and other commercial enterprises. The year is 2005.

Looking back just over one hundred years, the scene was very different. The road was little more than a sandy track, when it was the sound of horses hooves and cartwheels that could be heard, or footsteps of people as they walked from place to place. The whole area was a vast expanse of open countryside, a landscape of moorland scrub, forests, plantations and fields.

On this road to Mansfield a small cluster of houses formed the agricultural village of Clipstone. A village referred to by some, as 'Kings Clipstone' because of the ancient ruins of King John's Palace which lie in a field behind the houses.[1]

The ruins of King John's Palace

In 1900 the traveller would have left the village of Clipstone behind, and journeyed on the long open road towards Mansfield. Under foot the road would have been both sandy and rough. Eventually, the buildings of Newlands Farm could be seen down in the valley. In the surrounding fields, farm labourers would be seen working with a horse and plough, or gathering in the harvest, depending on the time of year.

Before long the private road to the Welbeck Estates would be reached. This was

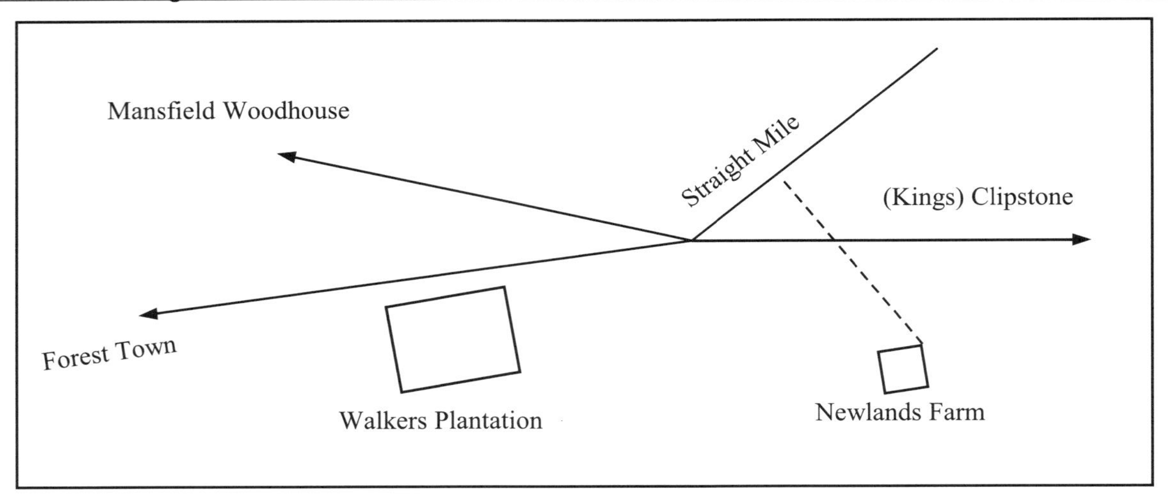

named Clipstone Drive where the unusual sight and noise of motor cars may well have startled some travellers. Often referred to as the straight mile it was where early car enthusiasts met and raced their automobiles.[2] Such a machine and pastime were beyond the means of the ordinary person of that time. Some would have found the noisy machines a terrifying sight, while others no doubt found it a thrilling experience.

For the traveller the journey to Mansfield continued past the trees of Walkers Plantation, and on towards a lone building built of grey stone aptly named 'The Travellers Rest.' The building, though changed a little in style, is still occupied today. While the date it was built has not been established, it is known to have been there in the mid 1800s when it was both a farm and a public house. The Travellers Rest was the property of the Duke of Portland's Welbeck Estate, and leased to various tenants until May 1945, when along with other properties it was sold.[3]

In the early 1900's, this isolated farmhouse with green ivy growing up the walls, a duck pond and large spreading trees, would have been a welcome sight and provided an opportunity for the traveller to take a rest.

Not too far beyond the Travellers Rest a crossroads was reached. The landscape was still open and often wild and windy. A road to the left meandered down past areas of woodland, leading on towards the village of Rainworth, and eventually the Minster town of Southwell. To the right, the road rose slightly before dropping steeply down Old Mill Lane, over the river Maun and on to the grey stone buildings of Mansfield Woodhouse. This lane, also known as Woodhouse Road, or Sheep Wash Lane, speculates on earlier activities and occupations of the area.

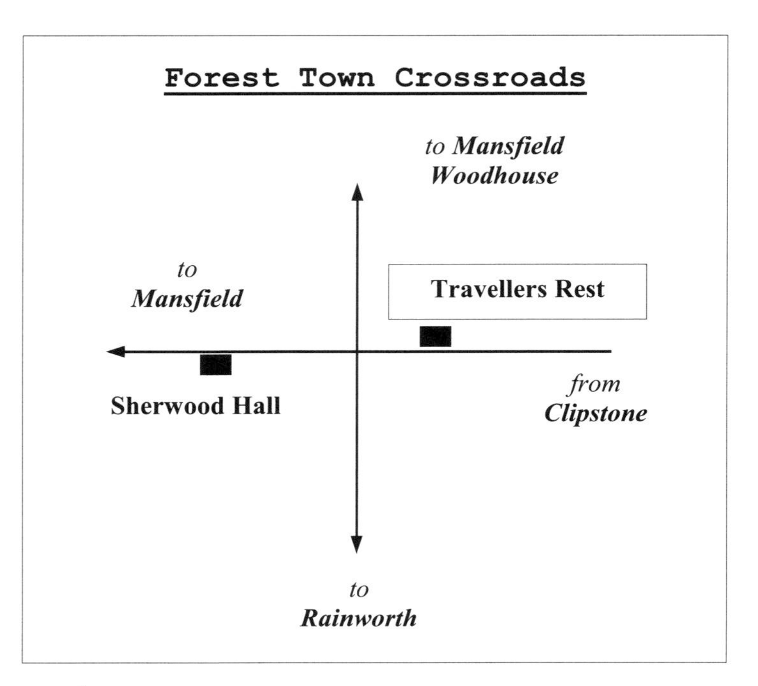

Continuing forwards at the crossroad, towards the town of Mansfield the road goes past the large splendid building of Sherwood Hall. This large house built of brick and stone with a slate roof had extensive grounds and farm buildings.

Surrounded by numerous trees Sherwood Hall dates back to at least 1800. Since then it has had many occupants, some were owners others just tenants. One of the first known was a Colonel Kellet.[4] The cotton spinner and race horse owner Thomas Holdsworth from Manchester was another.[5] William Wilson, a Nottinghamshire cotton spinner later resided there and eventually left for industrial Sheffield.[6] During the twentieth century, there were yet more occupants before the Hall was eventually demolished to make way for the school that now stands on the site.[7]

In the early years of the Travellers Rest and Sherwood Hall, local people would have been very aware of all the dusty roads, footpaths, and wide-open spaces. They would know the fields where many a rabbit could be poached to provide additional food for the cottage table. Many would have walked in areas of woodland, by streams and the river Maun, possibly catching a fish or two.

On cold windy days they would have discovered the road to Mansfield had little or no shelter, while on a fine summers day the views all around would have been something to behold, and the air would have been fresh and clean. It was an area of serenity and freedom, away from the noise and industry of the town of Mansfield.

However such serenity and freedom was not to last. By 1900 plans were already in progress to change the peace and serenity of the local countryside and devastating changes to the landscape were about to take place. The Bolsover Colliery Company was set to make its mark on the Nottinghamshire countryside and transform the area with modern enterprise. The search for coal became a priority.

Changes such as these were considered necessary for the progress of the country's expanding population and industry. As they developed, they wiped away the past and established a new era in the locality's history.

NOTES

1 These ruins are not accessible to the general public but can be seen from the road. It has been argued that an early name for the village was Kings Clipstone and this changed over time. Campaigners were recently successful in having the name reinstated.

2 Report and memories of the early speed trials on 'the Straight Mile'-Mansfield Chronicle Advertiser 20 Nov. 1969, & Welbeck Newsletter Issue No 8 Winter 1998.

3 The Clipstone Estate Sale Catalogue 10th May 1945.

4 The History of Mansfield and its Environs - W. Harrod

5 Kelly's Directory.

6 Mansfield Reporter 3 July 1914.
Anderson M. - *H.J. Wilson - Fighter For Freedom* (1953).

7 Saville House School occupied the Hall prior to it being demolished and Sherwood Hall School being built.

3 - LAND OWNER AND COLLIERY COMPANY

In nineteen hundred, one of the most prosperous men in the locality was the Duke of Portland, of Welbeck Abbey, near Worksop. He owned extensive land and property in many places including Nottinghamshire and Derbyshire.

The Duke's Welbeck estates were beneficial in numerous ways, and included providing many of his guests with leisure and sporting facilities such as shooting in the area around Clipstone. While much of the local land was green and fertile, encouraging agriculture and forestry on the estates, underneath it was rich with seams of dark black coal. The nation's demand for coal was increasing, and it gave landowners such as the Duke of Portland, a new option of supplementing their income. It was a time of new opportunity in which both land and colliery owners stood to gain. For the Duke of Portland, this coal was to become an additional asset. New colliery companies had already been founded and were prospering. One of these was the Bolsover Colliery Company whose founder member was Emerson Muschamp Bainbridge, a man who had become well known in mining circles during the latter part of the nineteenth century.

In 1889 after successful negotiations with the Duke of Portland he obtained a lease of the Top Hard, or Barnsley bed of coal under areas of Derbyshire and Nottinghamshire. He then founded the Bolsover Colliery Company to take over the lease, and mine the coal. It was the beginning of many productive years by the Bolsover Colliery Company.[1]

Appropriately, the company's first mine was sunk at Bolsover, Derbyshire, and coal was reached there in 1891. Eight years later in February 1889 the future of the company's second mine, also in Derbyshire, was secured when coal was reached at Creswell. At both Bolsover and Creswell, the Bolsover Colliery Company established new communities to accommodate the miners and their families. Communities that continued to grow as the collieries became established.[2]

The Bolsover Colliery Company continued to look for new opportunities to expand its coal fields, and ten years after Creswell was sunk, negotiations once again took place with the Duke of Portland. This resulted in the company obtaining the lease to work an additional area of Top Hard coal in the county of Nottinghamshire.[3] The year was 1899 and as the twentieth century approached, so did the planning, preparation, and sinking of the Bolsover Company's third colliery within a few miles of Mansfield. The new colliery was to be sunk near to the agricultural lands and property of Crown Farm. This was the beginning of the Mansfield Colliery, later to become known as Crown Farm Colliery or Crownie. It was also the birth of a new community, a community that was to be named FOREST TOWN.

NOTES

1 Marples P. Dissertation, Advanced Certificate in Local History 1994.
2 As above.
3 As above.

4 - THE 'GROUND RULES'
(The Colliery and Conservation)

Before either the Mansfield Colliery or the village could be developed, negotiations had to take place. The Bolsover Colliery Company had to consider all the long term possibilities; it had to look to the future and what could be gained. Likewise, the Duke of Portland had to ensure there were long term advantages in allowing the use of his land for coal mining purposes. The Duke would require royalties on the coal extracted (a percentage on each ton of coal). Additionally he was concerned for the conservation and management of the land, which he was leasing to the Bolsover Colliery Company.

Numerous letters and documents passed between the representatives and solicitors of the parties involved. Mineral rights were ascertained. The welfare of the farmers and tenants was an important consideration; both they and their property had to be respected. It was stated that they should be paid compensation for damages to their property, entry on to their land, and destruction of any crops. The safe protection of farm animals was also essential and the Colliery Company had to:

> *'fence off with good oak posts, and double rails, or with good single iron rails or hurdles in substantial like manner and in such a manner as to prevent cattle, horses, and sheep from straying and getting upon works or premises during any period either land or property was being used by the Colliery Company.'*[1]

The local environment was also considered, for it was stated that streams and watercourses had not to be polluted by rubbish, waste, sewage or any other poisonous noxious liquids or gases.

Trees could only be chopped down if they were growing in an area needed for colliery development, such as buildings or the construction of railways, tramways and roads. The trees should only be felled with prior agreement, (one calendar month after the Duke's land agent had been notified of their position). Likewise the existing footpaths had to be maintained and the Colliery Company had to try and prevent any new footpaths becoming established. Furthermore it was said that once the mine had ceased to operate, the land had to be reinstated, as near as possible to what it was, before the mining started.[2]

In agreeing to his land being leased and the new coal mine being developed, the Duke of Portland also made sure he exercised an element of control over the colliery workforce and consumers. Such people were referred to as the Bolsover Colliery Company's agents, workmen, labourers, servants and customers. The company had to endeavour that these people would obey the rules, keep to the footpaths, and not trespass.[3]

In those days the temptation of poaching off the land and fishing in the streams or lakes, would have been something that many men and boys succumbed to.

All these regulations written into the agreements had a bearing on how the Bolsover Colliery Company policed both their workforce, and the new village.

The key person, who negotiated with the Duke of Portland's agents regarding Mansfield Colliery and the new village, was John Plowright Houfton. He had a profound understanding of the needs of all people. This was gained from his father Charles Houfton, who himself had risen from humble beginnings to be a colliery manager in the Leeds area of Yorkshire. John was born at Chesterfield and educated at Eastwood, Nottinghamshire. He pursued a career in the mining industry and gained both experience and qualifications in Nottinghamshire, Derbyshire, Staffordshire and Yorkshire. In February 1890, he was appointed the general manager of the Bolsover Colliery Company and was instrumental in the company's future development and expansion.[4]

For John Plowright Houfton, the position of the general manager for the company was very much a pioneering one. He was responsible for virtually everything; this included consulting with the Duke of Portland's agents, and the sinking of the new colliery. He had the responsibility of dealing with the employees as well as overseeing subsidiary companies that were part of the Bolsover Colliery Company, such as farms, brickworks, and a stone quarry. His position with the company demanded respect, but in return, he also respected his workforce, and he soon became familiar with the people who lived and worked in the area around the Mansfield Colliery.

NOTES

1 NUHL PLN 505.
2 As above.
3 As above.
4 Brisco J.P. *Nottingham & Derbyshire at the Opening of the 20th Century.*

5 - THE FARMS

The area where Mansfield Colliery and its associated village were to be developed, contained two farms that were both strategic landmarks at that time. These farms, Crown Farm, and the Travellers Rest Farm are known to date back to the middle of the nineteenth century, possibly even earlier. Census returns reveal that the farms had various occupants from 1861. The Duke of Portland is believed to have owned the farms[1] and leased them to tenant farmers. Both farms situated in rural countryside soon became well known to all those involved with the planning and construction of the colliery and village.

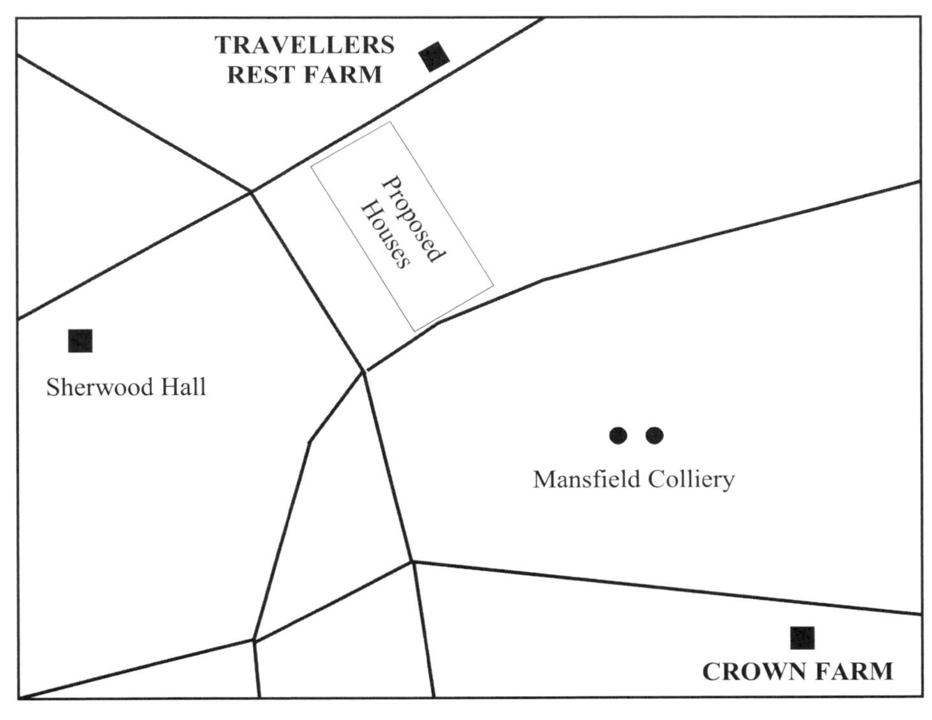

As the Mansfield Colliery Company sank their pit near to Crown Farm, the new colliery's official name was often forgotten, and it soon became known as Crown Farm Colliery or 'Crownie'. The farm itself was reached from the Eakring Road, where a long dusty track with brick lined dew ponds on the left, continued towards a stack yard on the right. At the end of the track was the farmhouse, a building that is recalled as having many rooms that were lit by paraffin lamps.

To the rear, separated by a wall, was the crew yard that had stables and a raised grain store. The farm implements were stored under the grain store. In the crew yard

Crown Farm

'mucking out' was done, and the accumulated manure was eventually spread over the nearby fields. A dairy and a pigsty were among the other outbuildings. To the front of the farmhouse, an earth closet was situated halfway down the garden.[2]

Horseradish was just one of the vegetables grown in the garden. Damson and russet apple trees grew in the orchard, and there were fruit bushes such as gooseberry, red and blackcurrant, these added to the self-sufficiency of the farm. In the long field known as 'the paddock', cattle grazed, and wild rabbits ran about in the grass, the farm children would sit making daisy chains as they watched. Around the farmyard, cackling geese strutted while a large gander was not always friendly to strangers. In the surrounding fields wheat, barley, mangolds and turnips were sown and later harvested.[3]

James Newton was the tenant farmer at the time Mansfield Colliery was being sunk. He was born into a farming family, and as a young man, served with the South Nottinghamshire Yeomanry.[4] On leaving the Yeomanry around 1894, he took over the tenancy of Crown Farm. His first wife Elizabeth (nee Hurst) died in January 1910 leaving him alone at the farm with three young sons, Frank(?), Leonard (born 1900) and George (born 1902), and daughter Lucy (born 1907). James remarried, to Edith Fox and twins Frederick John and Edith were born in 1910, and William (?).[5]

James Newton with Tommy the horse at Crown Farm

The farm nestling in the fields near to the Mansfield Colliery, became a familiar landmark to all who worked there. Likewise the disruption, noise and the colliery workmen soon became well known to James Newton and his young family.[6]

The Travellers Rest Farm, was across the fields from Crown Farm.[7] The first houses of the new colliery village were built in close proximity to this farm, and the houses were often referred to as 'the Colliery Cottages to be erected near to the Travellers Rest.'[8] Unlike Crown Farm which was reached by a long track, the Travellers Rest was built on the Ollerton to Mansfield Road and was easily accessible to any passing traveller. People could stop there to quench their thirst, for during the latter half of the nineteenth century, census returns show the building served both as a farm and a beer house. No doubt this is why it was named the Travellers Rest.

While most people calling at the Travellers Rest would have welcomed a glass of ale after walking along the dusty roads, not all customers were friendly. In 1858 the local newspaper reported a 'Disgraceful Assault on Landlady'. Two labourers Reuben Day, and John Howard of Mansfield were convicted for a disgraceful row at the Travellers Rest Inn, near Sherwood Hall. The landlady, Mrs Harvey was grabbed by her hair when she refused to draw beer for some customers unless they paid for it. They also upset tables, broke furniture and a large quantity of eggs.[9] Additionally the newspaper also records, 'the house is situate in a lonely spot and no immediate assistance could therefore be obtained[10].'

Interestingly the two men convicted were also known to the courts for poaching game on the Duke of Portland's land at Clipstone.[11] Rumour has it that the drinking licence for the Travellers Rest was taken away after the Duke of Portland discovered rabbits and hares poached from his land were being sold there. While no evidence has been found to validate this, there is no doubt a strong element of truth in the story.

The 1861 census shows George Harvey as the tenant, giving his occupation as 'Beer House Keeper.' His wife Mary and son Tom are also listed, Tom is a carter. By 1871 George has died and Mary his widow is recorded as 'Licensed Victualler' with her son Tom as a farmer.[12] While Mary Harvey, or at least her son Tom, were known to still be at the Travellers Rest in 1876,[13] by 1881, James Wright and his wife Mary had taken over the tenancy.[14] How long they remained there is unknown. By 1901 James Vincent and his family were the occupants of the Travellers Rest, they had previously lived just a few miles away on Berry Hill Road, an area then known as being in the parish of Lyndhurst.[15]

The Vincent's new home, the Travellers Rest was a grey stone building with foliage growing up the front wall. It was of a reasonable size with sitting rooms, a kitchen and scullery, plus four bedrooms.[16] Outside in the yard there was a water pump[17] and a building that housed the earth closet. Around the farmyard were pigsties, stables, cow houses, cart sheds and fodder stores.[18] In the surrounding fields big shire horses were a regular sight, as they walked up and down in front of the farmer and his plough.

The Travellers Rest circa 1910

Evidence of some of the outbuildings of the Travellers Rest Farm that could be seen in 1994

Despite being on a main highway, the Travellers Rest was still an isolated farm when James Vincent, his wife Eliza and their family moved there. However they soon became aware that everything around them was changing as Mansfield Colliery was sunk, and the building of the village began. Over the fields in the open countryside, the machines and buildings of the new colliery could be seen, while closer still, and only a few yards down the road from their home, rows of houses for the mineworkers were being built.

It was a time of great change, both the farms and their occupants were no longer remote. Within a short period of time they were to become part of an industrial area, and a village community, and for them it could possibly mean new prosperity if the people moving into the new village bought produce from their farms.

The lives of these local farmers and their families would have been a combination of hard work, with relative freedom as they enjoyed days of peace and tranquillity. Around them, the countryside would have echoed with the sounds of farm animals, birds in the hedgerows, and the gentle noise of cartwheels turning on the rough roads. This idyllic lifestyle would have quickly changed when men and machines moved into the area. The sinking of the colliery and the building of houses meant the local countryside was doomed to be reshaped, with the creative sounds of industry taking over from those of nature.

The development of the Mansfield Colliery and the new village with the inevitable rise in the local population meant for the Newton family of Crown Farm and the Vincent family at the Travellers Rest, life would never be the same again.

NOTES

1 To date no documentary evidence has been found to prove this.
2 Oral history John Newton, Forest Town 1993.
3 As above.
4 As above.
5 As above.
6 Mansfield Rugby Club is built on the land where the farm once stood.
7 The house and outbuildings, though no longer used for farming are still there today (2005).
8 NA DC/MW1/1/7 3 Dec 1901.
9 Midland Gazette 23 Oct 1858 p1.
10 As above.
11 As above.
12 RG10 3464.
13 Mansfield & North Notts Advertiser 19 May 1876 – Article 'Gross Cruelty to a Mare'.
14 RG311 311.
15 RG12 2657
16 NA SO IN 2/2/176.
17 Oral history P Langrick, present owner/land tax?
18 NA SO IN 2/2/176.

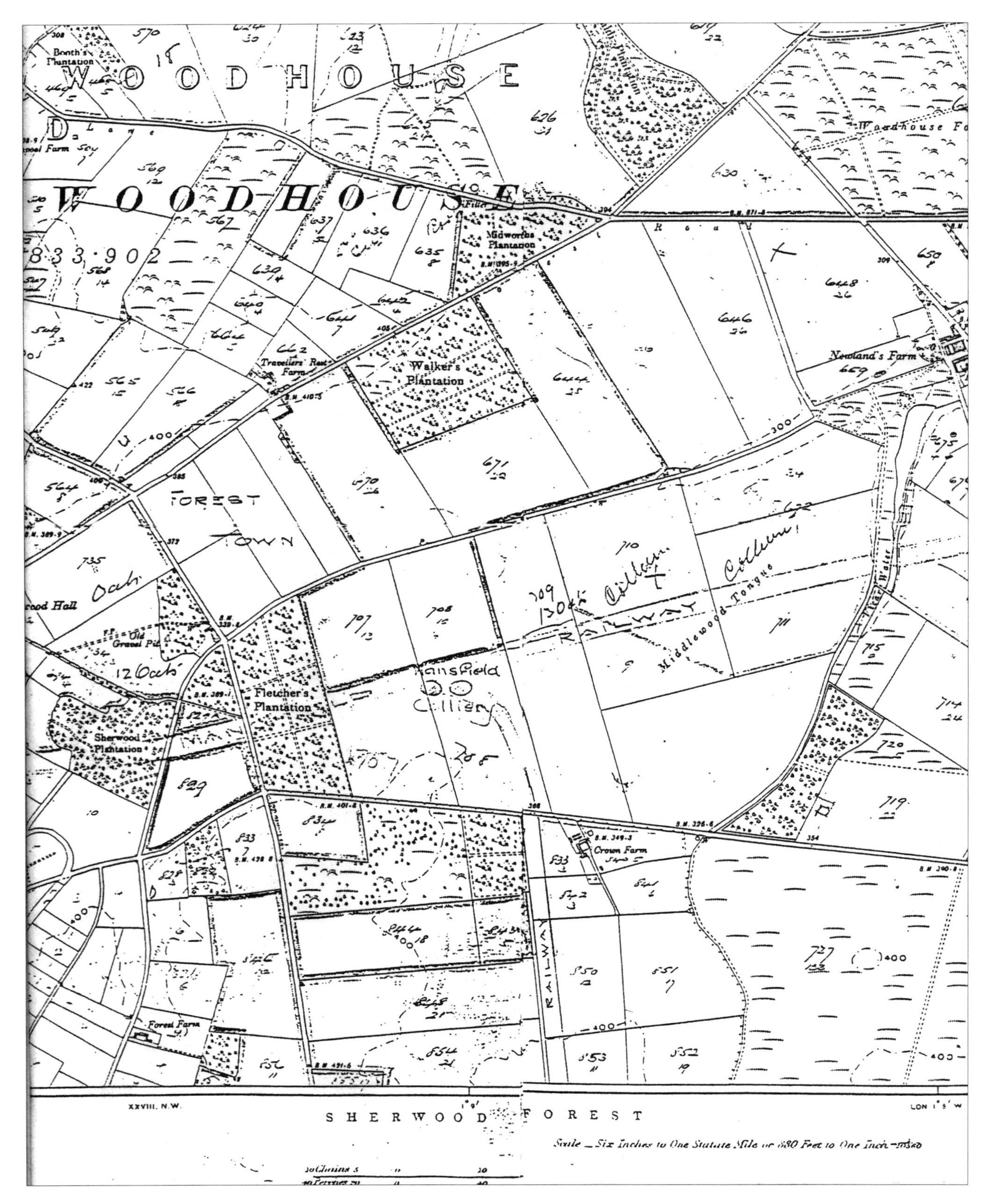

Map showing planning in progress

Ordinance Survey Map Second Edition 1900 Sheet No XXIII.SW Scale 6" to One Mile

6 - PLANNING THE COLLIERY AND THE VILLAGE

Before the sinking of the shafts for Mansfield Colliery commenced, a great deal of negotiating and planning with various authorities had to take place. Preparation work was required. Machinery and other equipment had to be taken to the site. Buildings, both temporary and permanent had to be erected. A railway link had to be established, and a workforce engaged. All this required financial support. Money for the Mansfield Colliery Company was raised by offering shares in the company.

Shareholders of the Bolsover Colliery Company[1] (the parent company) were offered shares in the new Mansfield Colliery. Early correspondence gives the price as 'One Pound a Share.'[2] How many people obtained shares in the Mansfield Colliery Company and who they were is unknown. It can only be surmised that they were people of reasonable wealth, who considered the new colliery a worthwhile enterprise.[3]

The planning and progress of the new venture was soon taking place. Architects, builders and local authorities were contacted, relevant plans were considered, and agreements both temporary and permanent were made.

Bolsover Colliery
Nr. Chesterfield.

Dear

Mansfield Colliery Company Limited

The Directors of the Bolsover Colliery Company Limited, (who are the promoters of the above Company) have instructed me to offer the Bolsover Shareholders, in the first instance, the whole of the Shares in the new Mansfield Colliery Company Limited, in proportion to their present holding in the Bolsover Company.

You are entitled to apply for..........................in the New Company. If you desire to have these or lesser or greater interest in the Company will you kindly fill up the form below and return it to me not later than the ...., together with a cheque for £1 for each Share applied for.

I am.
Yours faithfully
Secretary

Copy of letter in the Bolsover Colliery Company correspondence files deposited in Derbyshire Record Office.

In November 1901, Mansfield Woodhouse Council was written to regarding the erection of a bridge over the road from Crown Farm. In the following month, the council received a letter from Messrs Houfton & Johnson, Architects of Chesterfield regarding 342 houses that were to be erected in the parish. The letter referred to an enclosed tracing of the houses, saying the houses were to be built by Messrs Green Bros. and Sykes, and that a water supply was required.[4]

Terms for the new water supply had to be arranged, and initial negotiations took place with Mansfield Woodhouse Council and the Mansfield Town Council. In March 1902, Councillors Barlow, Simms and Warner were appointed as a sub-committee, to meet the owners of the 'Colliery Cottages' village, which was to be erected near the Travellers Rest.[5] The new cottages, were in fact the rows of terraced houses that became known as the Avenues. The purpose of the meeting between the council sub-committee and the owners of the 'village' was not just to discuss the water supply, but also who would be responsible for its cost. Mansfield Council estimated the cost of laying the water main along the Clipstone Road would be around £550.

Supplying water for the houses was not the only requirement discussed at the Mansfield Council meetings, a water supply was also required for the construction of the Bolsover Colliery Railway Branch Line. This became the topic of another debate, after it was reported in November 1902, that the contractors had laid a water main across a piece of land without being given permission.[6] Interestingly it was not until May 1903 the following year that the Bolsover Colliery Company inquired about a water supply to their new colliery near Crown Farm.[7]

For many years the new houses, (the Avenues) were a topic of regular discussion at the Mansfield Woodhouse Council meetings. In addition to arranging a water supply, the disposal of sewage and scavenging (household waste) was a necessary issue. The original proposal from the architects in 1901, was to adopt the septic tank treatment of the sewage. The builders were given permission in July 1904, to construct sumps for the temporary receipt of sewage from their properties in the new village.[8] However within a few months (October), the Sanitary Inspector reported to the Mansfield Woodhouse Council, that the emptying of the sewage tanks at the new village was a matter of concern. The builders were to be told the sewage tanks must be emptied at least once every seven days, and a deputation was appointed to confer with them about these arangements.[9]

By that time (1904) approximately 90 houses had been built. Just how many were actually occupied is unknown. However as building progressed and the village expanded so did the problem of sewage disposal. This issue continued to be a regular topic of the Mansfield Woodhouse Council meetings. In March 1908 the clerk reported that Councillors Palmer and Clatworthy, had spoken to the Duke of Portland's agent, who it seemed still objected to the sewage running on his Grace's land in the manner it was doing. However, it seems the agent did not wish to put the council in an awkward position, and suggested if the council would do the carting themselves, or get someone to enter into a contract for this, he (the agent), would provide land on which the sewage could be carted.[10] It is obvious that the council considered a more permanent solution was needed, for later that same year (1908) plans were underway to construct a Forest Town sewage scheme.

A third necessary requirement for the new village was the arrangements for scavenging, or as we know it today, refuse disposal. This too was another topical issue at the council meetings, for as early as May 1903, the builders, Messrs Green Bros. and Sykes were requesting that Mansfield Woodhouse Council should undertake the responsibility for the scavenging. The council obviously agreed, but who they employed to do this in the early years is unknown. However in January 1905 they accepted a tender of £10 from W.G. Limb, for the scavenging of Forest Town.[11] Despite this, the actual responsibility of providing dustbins for the houses, appeared to become an issue between the builders and the Bolsover Colliery Company. It was an issue that continued to cause problems for the Sanitary Inspector who in 1906, 1907 and 1908 had to issue seven-day final notices for the provision of bins to be complied with. No doubt this was a continuing problem as more houses were completed.

The whole area that was once fields and heath land was now undergoing a vast change. Advertisements offering land for sale appeared in newspapers as early as 1902. Freehold land to be sold by auction on the 30th October 1902 was stated to be,

> *'in close proximity to the Mansfield and Southwell Branch of the Midland Railway, and also to the colliery about to be sunk by the Bolsover Colliery Company. The vendors interest in the minerals will be included in the Sale.'*[13]

> ***THE NEW COLLERIES***
> *near Mansfield*
> *Several Lots of Eligible*
> ***BUILDING LAND FOR SALE –***
> *Apply Kings Athletic Stores Leeming Street, Mansfield.*[12]

This gave those with money the opportunity to speculate, look ahead and possibly increase their wealth.

One of the first speculators was James Hole & Co Ltd, Brewers of Newark, who purchased land in 1902. They were quick to apply to the Court Brewster Sessions re a licence for a Public House,[14] which they said was to be built on the Mansfield to Clipstone Road.[15] Despite their early application, Holes only operated an off-licence from 1908, at premises known as the Forest Town Stores. They planned to make this a fully licenced establishment when the need arose. It was not however until 1952 when this happened, and the building was converted into a public house and became 'The Prince Charles.'[16]

A brief mention has been previously made of the railway branch line, in the early development of the colliery and village. A railway connection to the colliery was important and when discussions took place between the Bolsover Colliery and the Midland Railway Companies it was stated that the colliery was to be sunk between Crown Farm and Newlands Farm.[17] (Though Newlands Farm is in the vicinity it is rarely mentioned in documentation concerning the colliery or village). By July 1902, an agreement had been made which said the branch line to the colliery would be a mile and a half in length and would connect with the Southwell Branch Line. Bridges had also to be constructed, and one to be erected over the road to Crown Farm was discussed by Mansfield Woodhouse Council in August 1902. Work on the new railway link started on the 28th July 1903, and the railway was soon scarring the landscape.

Not surprisingly, there would have been much speculation, also some controversy, as the various building projects and changes began in what was once a quiet locality. Throughout 1902 and 1903, various reports in respect of the new colliery and village appeared in the local newspapers. Inevitably all future eventualities were being discussed, and this even included anticipated accidents to the men who worked in the coal mines. It was considered that any such accidents would add to the work of the local hospitals, and because of this, the hospitals would need additional support and finance. As Sherwood Colliery was also being developed at this time, this meant a large increase in the working population of the area, and the hospital authorities cause for concern can be appreciated. Not surprisingly meetings between the local colliery managers, and the Mansfield and Mansfield Woodhouse Hospital authorities took place.

For some however, accidents and people's return to good health was not the only matter to be taken into consideration. Mr Robinson of Mansfield Woodhouse Council considered that they, (the council) should be planning one step further. He predicted that with a population of about a thousand to be housed in connection with the new Mansfield Colliery, all of them would need burying in due course! [18]

An early photograph of graves in St Alban's churchyard

Linked with all the early discussions and speculations was the major question, 'when would the actual sinking at the colliery begin.' There was much local guesswork as the initial work on the colliery site started, and the first houses were built. The engines, boilers, and other equipment were gradually erected, and eventually the sinking operations commenced on the first day of February 1904.[19]

The proposed new colliery and its related village were now a reality. In the once peaceful area of wide open spaces near Mansfield and Mansfield Woodhouse, a whole new way of life was being established.

NOTES

1 Mansfield Reporter 31 January 1890.
2 DRO Bolsover Colliery Co. Correspondence Files.
3 Very few letters and documents on the Bolsover Collieries have survived.
4 NA.DC/MW 1/1/7.
5 As above.
6 NA DC/M 1/4/37/4.
7 NA DC/MW 1/1/7.
8 NA DC/MW 1/3/9/2.
9 As above.
10 NA DC/MW 1/3/9/3.
11 As above.
12 Mansfield Advertiser 21/10/ 1902.
13 Rushcliffe Advertiser 24/10/1902.
14 NA Brewster Sessions.
15 Mansfield & North Notts. Advertiser 23/1/1903.
16 NA PS/B/30/9.
17 Mansfield Advertiser 11/7/02.
18 Mansfield & North Notts. Advertiser 6/3/1903.
19 The Courier 15/10/1910.

7 - SINKING
AND THE DISCOVERY OF COAL

Monday 1st February 1904, was a historic day in the history of Mansfield Colliery. This was the day the sinking of the shafts began, the day man and machine started a journey, digging deep into the bowels of the earth. The aim was to discover coal.

Prior to this date, a small amount of preparation in sinking the two shafts was first done by hand. The real work began when a pair of 30 inch steam winding engines was installed at each shaft, and sinking was brought into operation. The first 100 yards of digging was through bunter sandstone,[1] and the area around the site would have quickly taken on a rich colourful aspect as the sand was brought out of the ground. Even today, any change to the local environment, which involves the removal of topsoil, quickly reveals the golden sand that lies underneath this whole area.

After the sand, the excavation progressed through a vast amount of colourful geological strata, such as rock, pebbles, limestone and shale. There was red sandstone, yellow limestone, blue shale, grey rock, black bind and many others. Each layer varied in thickness as can be seen from the examples:

Limestone & marl in layers	4'	0"	[1220mm]
Coarse mottled sandstone	1'	0"	[305mm]
Blue shales	98'	7"	[30,048mm]
Brecca	2'	11"	[890mm][2]

Occasional narrow seams of coal were discovered[3] but these were insignificant. The real objective was to find a seam of rich black coal that could be worked for many years.

It is hard to imagine that the sinkers would have even considered the underlying beauty of the earth they were digging. The colour and texture of the sand, rocks, and pebbles would have gone unnoticed as the men worked in difficult and dangerous conditions. Water was an additional problem they had to contend with, and this was held back with cast iron plates, fifteen to each ring of the shaft, a method referred to as tubbing. Pumping water that contained sand was yet another difficulty that had to be overcome during the strenuous sinking operation at this mine.

Mansfield was the third colliery to be sunk by the Bolsover Colliery Company, and it was the most difficult. Problems that occurred during the sinking of the shafts at Mansfield, were far greater than those found at the company's first two mines at Bolsover and Creswell, both in Derbyshire. In those mines, there was no sand, and nothing like the quantity of water. It was said there was six times the amount of water at Mansfield [4]

At Mansfield, the Bolsover Colliery Company had taken the decision to do the sinking themselves. They felt they now had enough expertise and experience among their own employees to do this. John Plowright Houfton, the general manager said they had considered it 'important that the work in the shafts, through which the whole of the coal has to pass, should be carried out in the best possible manner.'[5] Many months later (after coal had been reached) he was reported as saying that the methods they used at the new colliery were very successful.[6]

However successful the methods used were, the work of sinking the shafts would have been extremely hazardous. The men did not have the safety helmets and the protective clothing that is worn today. It is difficult to imagine that they did not receive many cuts, bruises and experience accidents of some kind. However in those early days, only one minor injury was said to have occurred, that of a broken wrist. An accident which happened during the boring when one of the hammers working on a drill, slipped and caught the wrist of the man holding it. The fact that no major accidents occurred, was in stark contrast to the sinking of the nearby Sherwood Colliery when at least two men were killed.[7]

The Sinkers posing round the Shaft and in the Kibble, circa 1904/5

Despite the problem of water and sand it was not considered that there were any special complications involved with the sinking at Mansfield and the work made good progress.[8] Around 200 men were working at the colliery at this time; all were employed by the Bolsover Colliery Company. They worked under the direction of general manager John Bingley who had been with the Bolsover Company for many years.

Some of the men such as enginewright Tom Wakefield,[9] and William Cook, master sinker,[10] had previously worked for the Bolsover Company at their other two collieries. There would also have been others, men already well known to the company for both their skills and work.

Among the many men reputed to have been involved with the sinking were Albert Beresford, Charles Edward Shelton, Richard Fisher, the Bullock brothers, Martin Mannion and Willam Barlow.

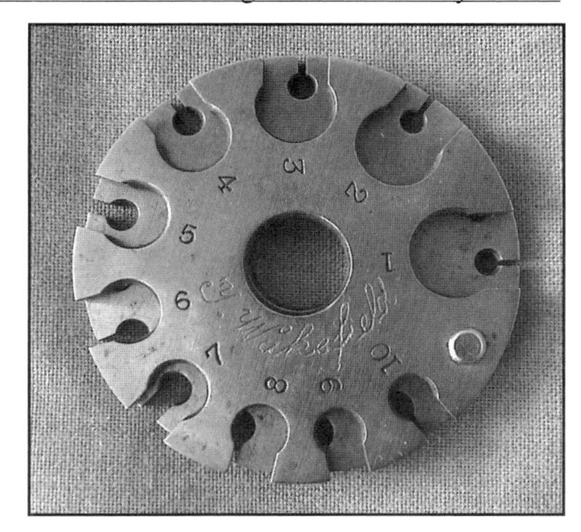

Wire Gauge belonging to the enginewright Tom Wakefield

The days would have been long and strenuous for the workmen who toiled in all types of conditions, and it was in the company's interests to look after their welfare. For this purpose, the Bolsover Company erected a temporary club for the men who all lived within the area of the new colliery.[11] They believed the provision of social recreation encouraged good working relationships, and in turn the work of the men would be more effective.

The period of the sinking would have been a nail-biting time for the colliery owners, investors, and the sinkers. So much depended on the discovery of an appropriate thick seam of coal, one that would ensure the future of the new colliery.

It was at the end of May 1905, when such a discovery was made. A seam of Top Hard coal five feet four inches [1625mm] thick was finally reached. This was only five inches [127mm] below a narrower seam of Coombe coal (house coal), the two seams could be worked together and it gave the equivalent of six feet four inches [1932mm] of coal.

The rejoicing and celebration at the discovery is not hard to imagine. Such a seam of coal was what everyone had been striving for, and it had only taken fourteen months to achieve.[12] John Plowright Houfton, general manager of the Bolsover Company told the newspapers;

> *"I think the fourteen months the sinking has taken must be nearly a record. Considering the length of tubbing we had to put in, and the amount of water we had to deal with, as well as the difficulty of pumping water with sand, it is certainly very good."* [13]

The discovery of this seam of coal now gave way to great anticipation that the pit would soon be in full working order and producing millions of tons of rich black coal. Two hundred and forty men were now employed at the colliery, and the number would gradually increase. It was anticipated there would be an additional two thousand once the colliery was in full working order. Already, the first houses had been erected and were being lived in by mineworkers, and their families. More houses

Mansfield Colliery

would soon be built. The village was already unofficially known as Forest Town, and now, along with the colliery it had a future.

The estimated life of the Mansfield Colliery was originally predicted to be fifty years. This was however underestimated and the production of the coal went on for 83 years from the date they found the coal in 1905 to its closure in 1988.

NOTES

1 Derbyshire Times 3 June 1905.
2 Extracted from 'Mansfield Colliery' in the Concealed Coalfield - Walter Gibson HMSO 1913.
3 As above.
4 Derbyshire Times 3 June 1905.
5 As above.
6 As above.
7 As above.
8 As above.
9 The Quarterly News July 1929.
10 Derbyshire Times 3 June 1905.
11 Derbyshire Times as above.
12 Derbyshire Times as above.
13 Derbyshire Times as above.

8 - THE AVENUES

As the sinking and the construction of the new Mansfield Colliery progressed, so did the building of the new village. This was a short distance away but still within sight of the colliery. Land that was once a long sloping field soon became covered in bricks, scaffolding, and other building material. The noise of the builders quickly became intermingled with noises of colliery activity.

The Bolsover Colliery Company believed in providing new permanent housing for their workforce and they built appropriate villages when they sank their coal mines. Not all colliery companies had this policy. Only twenty miles away at a new colliery in Dinnington (Yorkshire), both workers and their families lived in temporary accommodation of tin huts, which continued for many years.[1] The Mansfield Colliery miners were more fortunate, and they were encouraged by the prospect of decent housing. For them, rows of new terraced houses soon appeared on the landscape, houses which became known as 'The Avenues'.

The planning and preparation of the new village was underway by December 1901, when Architects Messrs Houfton & Johnson of Chesterfield, were in contact with Mansfield Woodhouse District Council. In the early years Forest Town was in the parish of Mansfield Woodhouse, and the architects were enquiring about a water supply for the 342 houses (often referred to as cottages), that were to be built in the parish. The correspondence from the architects refers to a tracing of the houses, which unfortunately has not survived.[2] One of the architects connected with this firm was Percy Bond Houfton, a nephew of John P. Houfton, the general manager of the Bolsover Colliery.

The actual date the building of the houses started is unknown but correspondence from the builders, Green Bros. & Sykes of Chesterfield began appearing in council minutes in 1903. In May they were applying for the scavenging, [refuse collection] for their new cottages near the Mansfield Colliery. This may have been a preliminary request, or it is more likely that some of the houses were already completed and were occupied by the men working on the colliery site. However in December that same year, the council were suggesting the builders should provide dustbins to the houses in the village,[3] so it can be assumed that several of the houses were definitely completed and occupied.

Building the houses required initial investment and financial support, and the Bolsover Colliery Company obtained investors from a very wide area. Contrary to popular belief that the Colliery Company owned all the houses, research has revealed otherwise. Blocks of houses in the Avenues were owned by numerous different people including:-

Henry Baldwin	London	*W. R. Clarke*	Loughton
L. J. M. Coates	London	*Rosa Harvey*	Colwyn Bay
Mrs E. M Bantock	Brighton	*Clare E. Spooner*	(no place given)
A. C. Sykes	Bolsover	*Mrs Wright*	Penrith, Cumberland[4]

The owners would have leased the houses to the Bolsover Colliery Company for a specified number of years,[5] and in turn the Colliery Company sublet to the miners and their other employees.[6]

The Avenue houses built in a long sloping field off the Clipstone Road, were Forest Town's first housing estate. They have always been known as 'The Avenues', because of the nine rows (avenues) of terraced houses, which are appropriately named First Avenue, Second Avenue, Third Avenue etc. This new colliery village enjoyed the distinction of having streets named in the American style. The long rows of houses were built of brick, and they had very tall chimneys, which soon prompted the nickname of 'Spiky Island'. The name is said to have originated when miners at the colliery looked back to the village, and they saw row upon row of long rooftops with tall chimneys. To them it looked like a 'Spiky Island.'

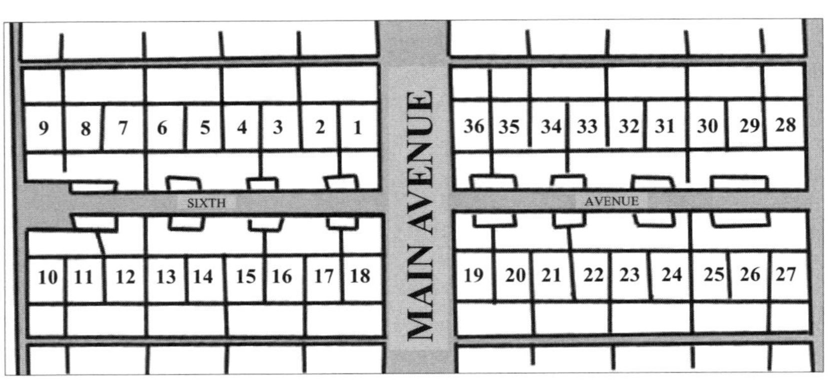

The Avenues are themselves an interesting feature, and fitting to the village name of Forest Town, can be contrasted to a large tree. Down the middle is the wide road of Main Avenue,[7] (the trunk), nine roads, (branches) are spread out on either side. The house numbering starts from the middle at Main Avenue, and proceeds anti-clockwise (1 - 9), continues over the road (10 - 17), crosses over Main Avenue (19 - 27), and returns back to Main Avenue again (28 - 36). This can be a little confusing, for even today finding your way on the Avenues is a challenge for people who are not familiar with the layout.

The building of the Avenues progressed over a number of years, the houses appear to have been built randomly a block at a time, rather than in consecutive rows. This may have been relevant to funding from appropriate investors/buyers for the properties, and can be compared to the building of new housing developments today.

Information from the 1910 Land Tax Survey, reveals, 1 - 9 Fifth Avenue owned by Clare Elizabeth Spooner, were completed in 1903. The remainder of the properties on that street owned by Charles Howell Hovey and the Chesterfield Estate Company are given as 1907. On Eighth Avenue numbers 28 - 36 were completed in 1904 but it was 1907/8 before numbers 10 - 27 were finished.[8] With so much ad hoc building, the Avenues would not have been a comfortable place to live in those early years. Once again it can be compared to being the first occupants on a new housing estate today, living on a building site when the construction of other houses is still in progress.

The first families moving into the Avenue houses discovered they were of a reasonable size. On the ground floor was a front room, kitchen, and scullery. There was a lobby entrance at the front and a pantry behind. Upstairs were four bedrooms, one was referred to as a box room because of its size. There was no bathroom, and the toilet (or closet) was situated outside in the back yard.[9] Lighting was by oil lamps,

The Avenue Houses under construction circa 1907/8

these hung from the ceilings. After a number of years gas was installed, and later on electricity which was generated and supplied by the colliery. Coal fires gave out a welcoming heat and provided the means to burn household rubbish. The chimney breast which ran through a bedroom, provided a minimum of warmth to that room.

Despite the dirty job of cleaning them with black lead polish, the huge cast iron fireplaces are still described and recalled with affection. 'They were a huge black lead affair, where the water was boiled at one side and an oven at the other.' 'The ovens still cooked the best rice puddings you could make.'[10] 'There was room for a pansion of bread rising on the hearth.'[11] For many years, the smell of home baked bread was a part of every day life. It greeted the children as they ran home from school for a slice of bread and dripping or jam.[12] The warm yeasty smell was a homely welcome to the miner when he came home tired and dirty from a hard shift at the colliery. There were no pit baths in those early days and he would have to wash the dirt from his hands and face at the kitchen sink before he ate his meal. The kitchen sink had just one tap for cold water.

At the front of the house was a garden, and at the back, a small asphalt yard with a coal house. When coal was delivered from the colliery, it was left on the street. Children used to help fetch the coal in and stack it, big lumps went at the front and the smaller pieces were thrown to the back. In the back yard, hanging on a nail was a tin bath ready for the weekly event. Bath night was quite an occasion in the miner's cottage when on the appropriate night of the week, the tin bath was lifted off its nail and carried into the house. It was then filled with water, cold water from the tap over the kitchen sink, and warm water taken from the boiler at the side of the fireplace. The family would then have a bath, one after the other in the same tub of water. The lack of hot water did not allow for a frequent change of bath water.

In the back yard, a pan closet (toilet) was housed in a separate brick building. This was a building that would not have been the most pleasant of places to linger in, no matter how well it was cleaned, as the contents of the pan could not be flushed away after each person had used it. The unpleasant task of emptying the pans had to be done manually by the 'night soil men.' They would lift up a flap at the rear of the toilet building and empty the contents into a cart. The smell would have been revolting, and it was not surprising that the night soil men wore masks to do this work.

Sketch of how the back yards in the Avenues may have looked with their tin bath and outside toilet.

When the night soil men came round, the village children had to be off the streets, but they would clamber to the bedroom windows and watch the proceedings from there. Just as today's children enjoy seeing dustbin lorries and the men who collect the household rubbish bins, the Forest Town children found it a fascinating event, watching the men going back and forth with their smelly cart.[13]

The outside toilets were also the object of mischievous children's pranks. It was not unknown for one child to act as a 'lookout' for unsuspecting people who visited the little brick building to answer the call of nature. The 'look out' would shout to his mates, "thuz one on number five." This was the signal to another child lurking in the street at the back of the building to lift the outside flap used for removing the pan and poke a stick into the hole, banging on the pan giving the occupant a nasty scare.[14]

The weekly rent paid by the first occupants of the Avenues was six shillings (30p) a week.[15] They looked after their property, swept their yards and had neat gardens. In those days they had to; the Bolsover Colliery Company had strict rules concerning its employees and tenants, including the one that said they could not have a dog. Today's elderly villagers recall this rule stood until a new policeman came along who had his own dog.[16] The tenancy of the houses was conditional on employment with the colliery, if a miner lost his job he also lost his home, and he had seven days in which to find new accommodation.

The Avenues and their first occupants were the pioneers of the Bolsover Colliery Company's new village. They came from near and far, places such as;

Mansfield, Creswell, Whitwell, Chesterfield,
Hucknall and Wakefield.

The Avenues circa 1907

The Avenues circa 1908

Among these people were the families

Swaby, Townroe, Jessop, Silcock
and Share
Murden, Swain, Cutts, Toplis, Bullock,
Moult, and Powell.

There were many, many more.

They were the people of the new village community. A community that grew to know each other, and to share their troubles, hardships, times of joy and happiness. They participated in many events that were part of the growth and the development of the village of Forest Town, often helping to raise funds and attending the special opening events. They donned their 'Sunday best' for those special occasions, and comfortable serviceable clothes for everyday wear. They were proud to live in the Avenues, it was the heart of the new village.

In front of 23 Fourth Avenue circa 1909
Left: Mrs Powell and children
Right: Mary Moult and her daughters Winnie and Nellie (standing)

NOTES

1. Marples P. Advanced Certificate in Local History Dissertation 1994.
2. NA DC/MW 1/1/7.
3. NA DC/MW 1/3/9/2 May & Dec 1903.
4. PRO IR58 55355 IR55356.
5. As above.
6. No documentary evidence has been found to confirm this.
7. Today (2005) when cars are parked either side and pedestrian calmers have been added, the wide perspective has been lost.
8. PRO IR58 55356. IR58 55355.
9. PRO IR58 55356. Oral history of elderly village people.
10. Oral history of elderly village people.
11. As above.
12. Dripping was the cold fat from the weekly joint of meat, it ran with rich meat juices, and was spread on bread.
13. Oral history of elderly village people.
14. Oral history from T. Redfern who recalled this story from his father, also from 96 year old Mr Naylor who remembered playing the game.
15. Chesterfield Courier 15 October 1910.
16. The village had a 'Pit Bobby' employed by the colliery, also a policeman from the local constabulary.

9 - ST DAVID'S MISSION THE FIRST ANGLICAN CHURCH

At the beginning of the twentieth century, going to church was a part of everyday life, and the parish registers of St Edmund's Church in Mansfield Woodhouse reveal where some of the first people to live in Forest Town went. However, as the new village of Forest Town started to grow, the need for establishing places for people to worship in the village itself became important, and in 1905, the Duke of Portland gave Forest Town its first Anglican church. This was erected near to the crossroads on the corner of Old Mill Lane, and the Clipstone Road. It was named St David's Mission Church.

It was appropriate that the new church stood near to Old Mill Lane, the road that led to Mansfield Woodhouse, for both St David's Mission and St Alban's the second Anglican church built in 1910-11, were both under the Parish of Mansfield Woodhouse until 1936.

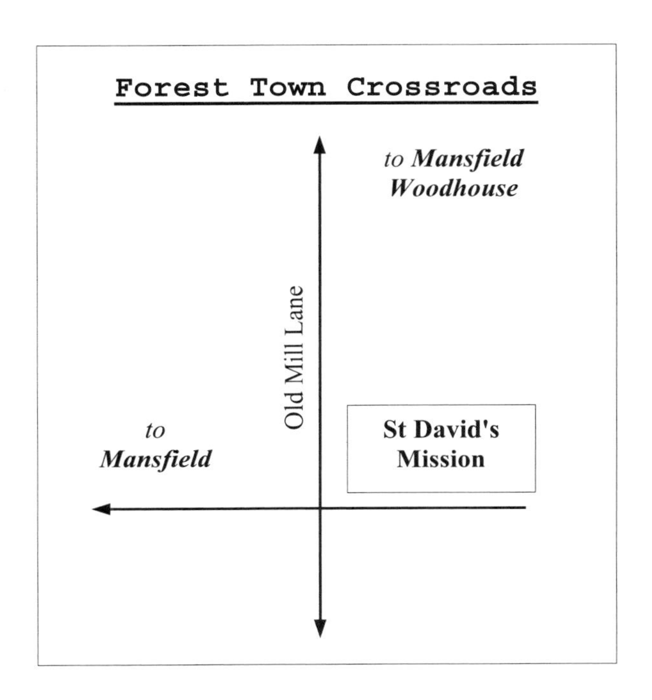

St David's Mission Church, was surrounded by a mixture of hedging and wooden fencing. The congregation entered through a wooden gate with a double notice board, which advertised the weekly services. On the outside of the building, a single lamp hung on the wall, providing a warm welcome on a dark winter's night. Just as today, people were called to the service by the ringing of a solitary bell, this was situated on the church roof and the bell rope ran from the roof down the outside wall.

The church, built of wood and corrugated iron could accommodate a congregation of 130 people who sat on rows of wooden chairs. Oil lamps were suspended from the roof and provided illumination, and music was played on a small organ that stood at the front.

On Friday 3rd March 1905, a dedication service was held which Rev. C. Webb, vicar of Mansfield Woodhouse and Rev. W. H. Foster, conducted; the organist and choir from Mansfield Woodhouse Parish Church took part. Hymns were sung from the Ancient & Modern Hymn Book.[1]

Arrangements were made for two services to be held each Sunday with Captain Cunliffe of the Church Army to be responsible.[2] Little is known of Captain Cunliffe and it is surmised he did not stay for very long at the Forest Town Mission Church or

St David's Mission Church circa 1905

Inside the Mission Church

in the area. In August 1907 a local newspaper reported him returning to Mansfield Woodhouse for a short holiday, during which time he took part in both a children's service and an evening service at St David's Mission Church in Forest Town. A Captain Tomlinson was believed to have been in charge of the church then.[3]

By February 1908 there was once again a vacancy at the tiny church, for at a meeting of the Nottinghamshire Church Extension Society, the Canon Prior of St Peter's Mansfield spoke of the spiritual needs of Forest Town. He said that there was a population of around 2000 and 'Forest Town presented a magnificent opening for a young man to work in.'[4]

Rev. Harry Bull was the curate that soon took up this challenge, for in the April of that year (1908) the local newspaper reported on the Easter services at the Mission Church it stating, 'the workers were pleased to have a visit by the new Vicar.'[5] Rev Bull who had previously been at St Lawrence's Church in Mansfield was therefore already familiar with the changes the local coal mining had brought to the area. Both he and his wife Margaret became ardent workers in the village for many years.

Margaret Bull

In 1909 the Mission was known to have a football club, (see the picture below). Mrs Bull held sewing classes for both women and girls, who all worked hard for the bazaars and sales of work. By 1910 the number of girls in the class had reached sixty.

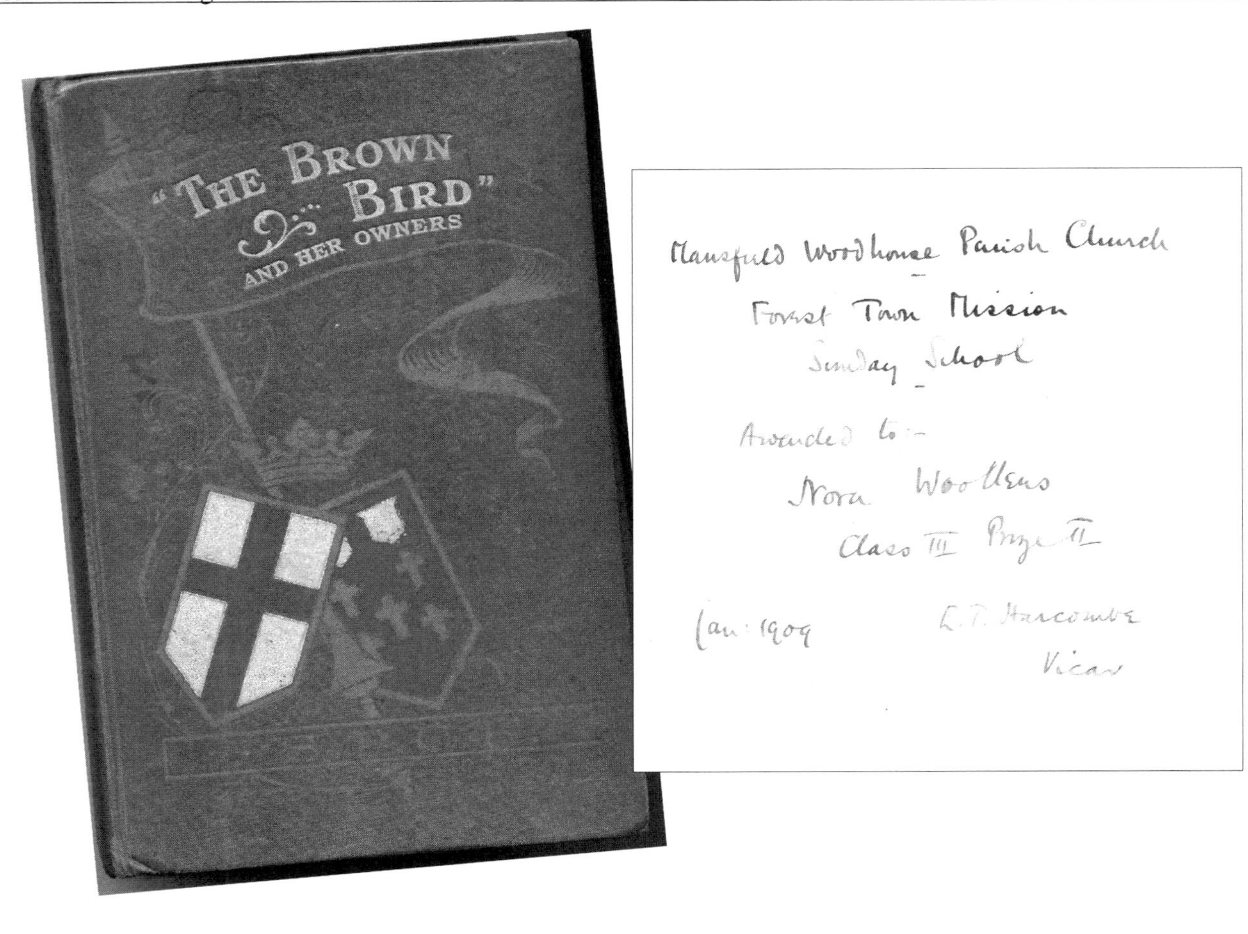

As in many churches, young people were encouraged to attend Sunday School and were rewarded for good attendance with a prize which was normally a book. In 1909 Norah Woollens received a book entitled 'The Brown Bird and her Owners' by Edith Cowper. The title of the blue covered book is in gold with shields decorated in red, white and gold. The inscription on the inside cover, written in ink says:

Mansfield Woodhouse Parish Church, Forest Town Mission Sunday School,
Awarded to Nora Woollens Class III, prize II,
Jan 1909, E. T. Harcombe Vicar

Within the church itself, there was evidence of pride and devotion by members of the congregation who made gifts for the enrichment of the sanctuary. From working men and women this represented a spirit of self sacrifice,[6] a devotion that continued when the need for a new church arose.

With an increasing population, it soon became evident that the little Mission Church was no longer adequate to accommodate the people of Forest Town. There were times when there had not been enough room for the Sunday School, and the Bible Class, and at the end of 1908, a fund was established to build a new church. The Duke of Portland once again showed his generosity by giving one acre of land to site both the church and a parsonage. In addition, he gave the sum of £2,000. The Bolsover Colliery Company gave a donation of £600 and said they would contribute annually to the curate fund. The village people were greatly encouraged and began organising fund-raising events. The newspapers were keen to report on these;

February 1909

Over 200 people were present at a Whist Drive and Dance on behalf of the Church Building Fund in the Council Schools.
Forest Town Orchestral Band played for dancing.
MCs were W. Kingston and C. Collier.
Mr J. Bingley distributed prizes won in the Whist Drive.[7]

This was an age before radio and television, and fund-raising activities were some of the main social activities of the time. Events such as whist drives, dances, concerts, and bazaars brought the local community together as they worked hard to raise money for their new Anglican Church. The little Mission Church had served them well, but now it was time to build a new and more permanent church building for the growing population to worship in.

However the doors of St David's were not to close, for once the new stone church was built, the wooden church building continued to serve the community as the Parish Rooms (Church Hall) for at least another 50 years for both social and welfare events. It was eventually demolished in the 1960's.

NOTES

1 Mansfield & North Notts Advertiser 10 March 1905.
2 Not to be confused with the Salvation Army.
3 Mansfield & North Notts Advertiser 23 August 1907.
4 Derbyshire Times 22 February 1908.
5 Mansfield & North Notts Advertiser 24 April 1908.
6 Mansfield & North Notts Advertiser 22 July 1910.
7 Mansfield & North Notts. Advertiser 26 February 1909.

10 - ST ALBAN'S CHURCH

Louis Ambler FRIBA, of Temple Chambers, London was the architect asked to design the new Anglican church to be built in Forest Town. He soon had to modify his original designs for the new church due to a lack of finance. Despite the substantial donations and fund-raising by people of the village, this still fell short of the sum required. Understandably, this was a topic of some discussion between the various people who were associated with the building of the church, and for Louis Ambler this must have been a very challenging time. When it was necessary for him to visit this area he stayed at Langwith Lodge, which was approximately four miles from Mansfield Woodhouse, the home of Mr Warner Turner, the Duke of Portland's agent.[1]

From 1908, a great deal of correspondence was generated over the building of both the new church and a house for the clergy known as the parsonage. Letters and plans passed between Mr Warner Turner, the Duke of Portland, Rev. Harcombe vicar of Mansfield Woodhouse, Bishop Edwyn, Southwell, other clergy, the architect and the ecclesiastical commissioners in Westminster. In addition there was necessary communication between the builders, clerk of works, and various suppliers. Even the local farmer Mr Vincent, from the Travellers Rest was not to be left out. Each one, in some way was involved with the building of the new church and the parsonage.

Numerous options were considered as to what could, or could not be done. Money was always an issue. Mr Warner Turner, told Rev Harcombe that he had seen the bishop, and they had discussed the matter of building the church. The bishop was in agreement that they should cut their cost according to their means.[2] Additionally it was suggested that the church should only provide the accommodation for the necessary population, with provision being made for the church to be easily enlarged when this was required.[3]

Eventually in July 1910, the foundations of the new church were laid and the building work progressed. A special memorial stone was placed in the east wall of the building, and arrangements were made for the Duke of Portland to perform the official stone laying ceremony on Saturday 5th November 1910.[4]

The cost of this stone £6-12s-10d (£6.64) was additional to the original building quotation.

The day, which started bright and sunny, was one of celebration. A special platform, which cost £2.15s 0d (£2.75), was erected for the occasion.[5] Clergy and choir were situated at one side, while invited guests were placed at the other. A centre space was left for the speakers, among them the Duke of Portland, who was making his first public appearance in Forest Town, Rev. E. T. Harcombe, (vicar of Mansfield Woodhouse), Harry Bull (curate in charge of Forest Town) and Mr A. Davis (Bolsover Colliery Company). On his arrival the Duke was saluted by a guard of honour that consisted of;

150 members of Forest Town Boys' Brigade
under Captain Bingley, Lieut. J. Senior,
Lieut J. Hinton, and Sergt. Major J. Lacey (instructor);

80 members of the St John's Ambulance Brigade
in the charge of Supt. A. Davis, First Officer Swaby, Second Officer Munks
and Third Officer J. Severn;

56 members of the Cadet Corps
under Lieut. Kingston and Lieut. P. W Houghton;

The Silver Prize Band was also present under the conductorship of
Bandmaster J. Cupit. [6]

The event was a joyous occasion. Large crowds of people from Forest Town, Mansfield, and elsewhere watched as Mr Louis Ambler, the architect of the church, presented the Duke of Portland with a silver trowel. First the Duke laid the mortar, then with a mallet he tapped the stone, and declared it well and truly laid. He continued by saying,

"In the faith of Jesus Christ we place this foundation stone, in the
name of the Father and of the Son and of the Holy Ghost, Amen." [7]

Hymns and prayers followed, and the ceremony concluded with the singing of, 'Oh God our Help in Ages Past', as the procession returned to the mission room.[8] The Duke inspected the Guard of Honour, and then tea for approximately 300 people was served in the Drill Hall. The day concluded with a dance and social at which the St Alban's Glee Club entertained.[9] The village community could rejoice the church was now being built.

The new church was to have a nave, chancel, sacristy, clergy vestry, choir vestry and organ chamber. The external walls of the church were to be of Bulwell stone with Weldon stone dressing, the interior to be lined with bricks and plastered. Ancaster stone was to be used for the columns and red Broseley tiles for the roof. The roof itself was fir and stained brown. Oak was chosen for the outer doors and Canary whitewood for those inside the church. Louis Ambler designed a font made of Ancaster stone to be situated at the west end of the nave, and he also designed and made the oak pulpit.

Plans for the north aisle and morning chapel were deferred to reduce expenditure.

The Stone Laying Ceremony 5th November 1910
Everyone was out in their 'Sunday best'.

The Duke of Portland making a speech. Note the camera man centre back.

(The north aisle was eventually built in 1936, but the morning chapel has never been built).[10]

The contractor for building St Alban's Church was
Charles J. Vallance and Sons.

Door Hinges & Furniture	*Jones & Willis Ltd*
Clergy Choir Seats & Pews	*Thomas Ullathorne*
Wood Block Flooring	*The British Flooring Co*
Wrought Iron Gas Fittings	*J. W. Singer & Sons*
Heating	*Thomas Danks & Co Ltd*
"Coal Port-Brosley" Tiles	*William Exley & Sons*
Ancaster Stone Font	*Bowman Bros.*[11]

A summary of the building account dated June 1911 shows the total net cost for the church was £3,404-17s-5d. (£3,404.87). A separate account reveals that for his work in preparing sketch plans, specifications etc Louis Ambler the architect was paid £287-17s-0d, (£287.85) this included £29-17s-0d (£29.85) for travel and other incidental out of pocket expenses.[12]

For the coal mining community of Forest Town the new church cost a lot of money. Despite all their fund-raising prior to the stone laying ceremony, in May 1911 the people of the village were still £300 short of the £600 amount they had promised to raise towards the building.

In an effort to reduce their liability, a two-day bazaar was held at the Drill Hall. Mrs Warner-Turner opened this event and was presented with a bouquet by Kathleen Bingley.[13] The stalls were varied and came under the heading of groups or the type of items they sold and included:

MOTHERS SEWING MEETING,
FLOWERS, VARIETY,
YOUNG LADIES, CHURCH OFFICERS,
ORIENTAL, PAWN SHOP.

Among the stall helpers were

Mrs O J Bainbridge	*P. Barker*	*A. Beresford*
H. Bull	*J. Bingley*	*I. Bloor*
H. Commons	*Mrs A. Davis*	*J. Guylor*
J. Hallam	*Mrs W. Holland*	*W. Kingston*
Miss F. Lacey	*Mrs T. Landers*	*Miss M. Murden*
W. Rose	*Mrs W. Rudge*	*Mrs T. W. Share*
C. W. Swaby	*W. Tebbutt*	*Mrs T. Wakefield*
Miss M. Whitney	*Nurse Willings*	*Miss I. Winter*

Refreshments were looked after by: Mesdames C. W. Swaby, F. Annable, P. Barker, H. Commons, W. S. Cooke, W. H. Cooke, G. Smith, W. Birkett, J. Barfoot, and Mr & Mrs A. Annable were in charge of 'Ices.'

The two-day bazaar raised a further £120 helping to reduce the outstanding debt towards the building fund.[14]

The building of St Alban's Church progressed and within two months of the fund-raising bazaar the community was once again uniting in a very special ceremonial event, the consecration of their new church.

This took place on Sunday 2nd July 1911. It was a day full of great rejoicing and celebration. In the morning the Bishop of Southwell, clergy and churchwardens, Messrs R. Dent and W. Pogmore, formed a procession to the church where upon being requested by the churchwardens, the Bishop consecrated both the building and burial ground.

In the afternoon a further ceremony took place when the Bishop consecrated the font and internal fittings.

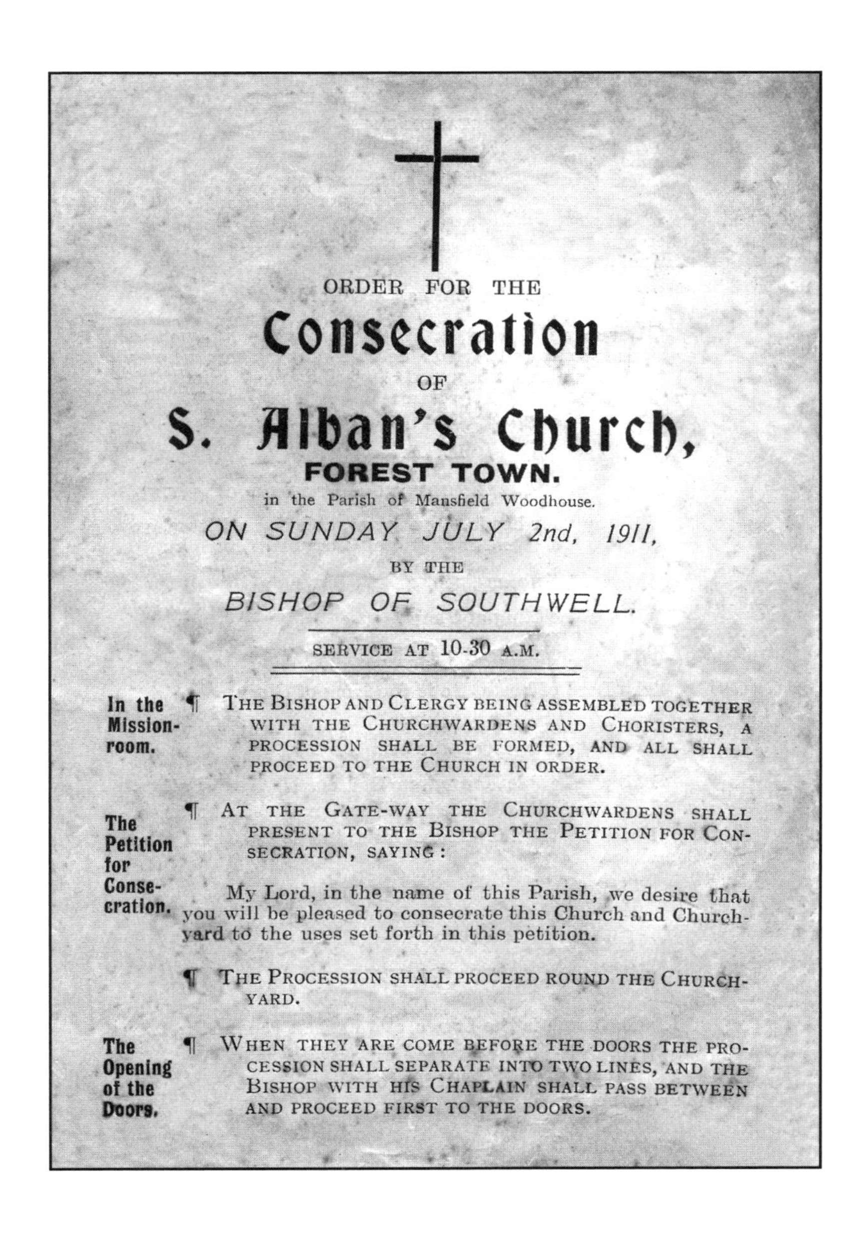

ORDER FOR THE

Consecration

OF

S. Alban's Church,

FOREST TOWN.

in the Parish of Mansfield Woodhouse.

ON SUNDAY JULY 2nd, 1911,

BY THE

BISHOP OF SOUTHWELL.

SERVICE AT 10-30 A.M.

In the Mission-room. ¶ THE BISHOP AND CLERGY BEING ASSEMBLED TOGETHER WITH THE CHURCHWARDENS AND CHORISTERS, A PROCESSION SHALL BE FORMED, AND ALL SHALL PROCEED TO THE CHURCH IN ORDER.

The Petition for Consecration. ¶ AT THE GATE-WAY THE CHURCHWARDENS SHALL PRESENT TO THE BISHOP THE PETITION FOR CONSECRATION, SAYING:

My Lord, in the name of this Parish, we desire that you will be pleased to consecrate this Church and Churchyard to the uses set forth in this petition.

¶ THE PROCESSION SHALL PROCEED ROUND THE CHURCHYARD.

The Opening of the Doors. ¶ WHEN THEY ARE COME BEFORE THE DOORS THE PROCESSION SHALL SEPARATE INTO TWO LINES, AND THE BISHOP WITH HIS CHAPLAIN SHALL PASS BETWEEN AND PROCEED FIRST TO THE DOORS.

The day came to a rousing end with the evening service when Archdeacon Richardson conducted 'a powerful sermon', and the well-known tenor, Morgan Kingston sang a solo 'in a masterful voice.'[15] The day was certainly one to remember for the people of Forest Town.

St Alban's Church was now ready for the people to worship in. Rev. Harry Bull was the first incumbent and remained at the church until 1924. Additional to the regular services, the new church could now be used for baptisms and burials, and it had its own registers, although until 1936 it still came under the parish of Mansfield Woodhouse.

The photograph above was possibly taken in 1911 around the time of the consecration. The Mission church can be seen to the left of the picture just behind the new church porch.

Below an early photograph of the church interior.

Since 1909 baptisms had taken place in the Mission Church but they had additionally been entered in the Mansfield Woodhouse registers.[16]

Some of the first entries in the new St Alban's Baptism Register were:

Annie Hardy	*12th September*	*1909*
Walter Cupit	*12th September*	*1909*
Phyllis Edith Needham	*3rd October*	*1909*
Olive Bolland	*3rd October*	*1909*
Alice Annie Murden	*3rd October*	*1909*
Alfred Thorn	*3rd October*	*1909*
Henry Alonzo Albon	*3rd October*	*1909*

The first page of the burial register contains eight entries, and sadly five of these were children.

BURIALS in the Parish of Mansfield Woodhouse (S. Alban's, Forest Town) in the County of Nottingham in the Year 1911 & 12

Name.	Abode.	When Buried.	Age.	By Whom the Ceremony was performed.
Vera Arrowsmith No. 1.	Forest Town	July 29th	4 months	Harry Bull
Ethel Sutton No. 2.	Forest Town	Aug. 19	4 months	Harry Bull
Thomas Frederick Bennett No. 3.	Forest Town	Aug. 31st		Harry Bull
Joe Barker No. 4.	Forest Town	Sept 4	7 months	Harry Bull
John Wilfred Cadwallader No. 5.	Forest Town	Sept 9	4 years	Harry Bull
Mary Ann Oates No. 6.	Forest Town	Nov. 28	39 years	Harry Bull
Sidney Ayres ~~Mary Ann Oates~~ No. 7.	Forest Town	1912 Feb 3	7 weeks	Harry Bull
James Walter Brown No. 8.	Forest Town	Feb. 5	16 years	Harry Bull

[17]

Soon headstones with carved names and inscriptions began appearing in the churchyard, it was the last resting place for many local people.

It is unknown what musical facilities the church had in the early years, they may have used the little organ from the Mission Church or the talent of people in the congregation who could play an instrument. For special occasions the colliery band could provide music to sing hymns to. However by 1917 the church were making plans to install an organ, and a design by Brindley & Foster was submitted in May 1917 at a cost of £515. This was accepted and the work began. The wonderful musical tones were soon to be heard, it was a great asset to the church.

(Original document in Nottinghamshire Archives PR 21,174).

On the 2nd December 1918, when the population of Forest Town had increased to around 3000 people, St Alban's Church was licensed for marriages. People could now marry in their own village and not have to go to Mansfield Woodhouse. The Anglican church in Forest Town was now firmly established and was able to provide fully for the needs of the expanding local community.

NOTES

1 NA PR21 155. Langwith Lodge was later used as a Diabetic Clinic, in 2005 it is a residential home for the elderly.
2 NA PR21 155.
3 As above.
4 As above.
5 As above.
6 Mansfield & North Notts Advertiser 11 November 1910.
7 As above.
8 St David's Mission Church.
9 Mansfield & North Notts Advertiser 11 November 1910.
10 As above.
11 The Modern Building Record Vol 3 - L Jones 1912.
12 NA PR21 155.
13 Mansfield Chronicle 11 May 1911.
14 As above.
15 Mansfield Reporter 7 July 1911.
16 The early registers for Baptisms. Marriages and Burials can be found in the Nottinghamshire Archive Office.
17 This was copied with permission of Rev R Smith before the register was deposited in the Nottinghamshire Archives.

11- THE METHODISTS

The Primitive Methodist Chapel

Some of the families moving to the new Forest Town village were of the Methodist faith, and they were quick to establish a place where they could meet together and worship. Their meetings were initially held in the home of a miner, Joseph Share.[1] A local newspaper reported in 1905, that the meetings were 'well attended, in fact crowded out.'[2] This situation obviously encouraged Methodist circuit officials to erect an appropriate building for Primitive Methodist worship, and they decided to build a school chapel that would accommodate 300 people.

The land on which the chapel was to be built was adjacent to the Travellers Rest Farm, and it was purchased from Holes the Brewers of Newark. The Brewers had previously acquired the land when the village was first being planned, they were no doubt anticipating a time when they would build a public house in the area.

When the Brewery re-sold the land they were very astute and made sure they looked after their own interests, for the relative document included the words 'and that no public house or building for the sale of beer wine or spirituous liqueurs shall be erected thereon.'

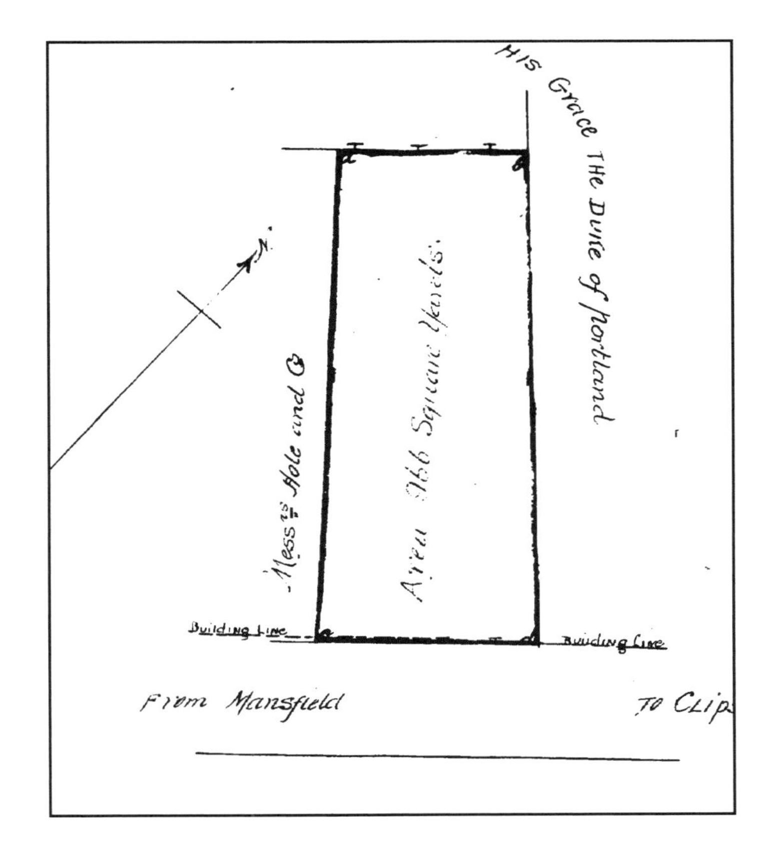

Plan with conveyance showing site purchased.

The conveyance and indenture for the land reveal the names of the first trustees for the new chapel,

William Kirk	*Mansfield - Assurance Superintendent*
Albert William Smith	*Mansfield Woodhouse - Assurance Superintendent*
Leonard Harvey	*Mansfield - Assurance Agent*
William Robinson	*Mansfield Woodhouse - Labourer*
Reuben Tebbett	*Mansfield Woodhouse - Miner*
Arthur Rutland	*Mansfield Woodhouse - Printer*
Joseph Share	*Forest Town - Miner*
Josiah Slack	*Forest Town - Miner*[3]

also *Reverend Michael Laycock*, Superintendent preacher of the circuit.

It was these trustees who agreed to the purchase price of two hundred and forty pounds ten shillings (£240.50), for land that was so important to the future of the Methodist worshippers in Forest Town.

With the land purchased, preparations began, and Mr F. P. Cook was chosen as architect of the new building. A ceremony to lay the foundation stones took place in the afternoon of Saturday 25th March 1905. Those special stones can still be seen today and were laid by:

Mr W. Robinson (on behalf of the trustees)
Miss Cook (Mansfield Woodhouse)
Mr Issac Smith and family
Mr Stewart (on behalf of the Mansfield Colliery)

Six smaller stones were laid by:

Mr Parkinson, Misses Parkinson
Mrs Rouse, Misses M. and F. Wakefield
Misses E. & F. Bingham
Fourteen bricks were laid by scholars[4]

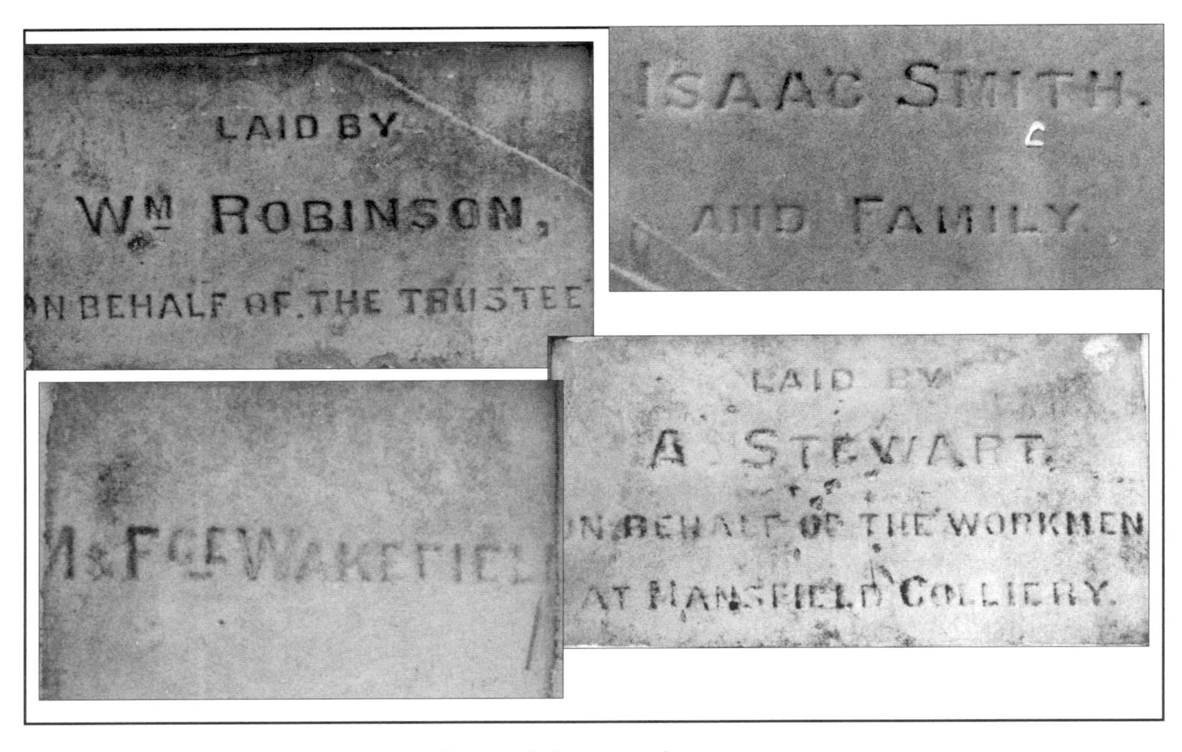

Some of the named stones

After the joyful stone laying ceremony, a tea for 170 people was held in the specially prepared barn of the Travellers Rest Farm.[5] A public meeting followed where people were encouraged to make donations towards the cost of the new chapel/ school room.

The building once completed was to have three vestries, an assembly room, and would accommodate 300 people. It was sited well back from the road as it was anticipated that once the need arose, a chapel itself would be erected in front of the schoolroom. Plans to do this were made, but were postponed when war broke out in 1914, and consequently the new chapel was never built.[6]

Work on the new building in 1905 made rapid progress, and within weeks of the special stone laying ceremony on the 25th March, the new chapel school was built, and ready to be officially opened. This took place at the end of May, and once again it was a time of great celebration. The Borough Band marched from the market place in Mansfield all the way to Forest Town. The dust stirred up by the marching feet would have been of little concern, as music of the brass band added to the excitement of the waiting people. The procession first went round the village before arriving at the new brick building where there was much singing. Mrs William Smith of Mansfield Woodhouse, 'a loyal supporter of Primitive Methodism'[7] unlocked the new chapel door saying that she hoped that this new place of worship would be a blessing for the neighbourhood.[8] After the ceremony, an open-air service was held. The new chapel was then thrown open for inspection, and the preparation of tea.

Two hundred people were there for the tea and additional musical entertainment by the band. An evening meeting followed at which Mr Kirk presided and various people including Mr W. Robinson, Mr L. Harvey, and Mr A. W Smith made speeches. The events of the day were considered to have been very successful, and had raised a further £10 of much needed funds. The cost of the new building had been estimated at £650 and so far only £60 had been realised. However the Primitive Methodists were undeterred, and the news that a rich seam of coal had just been discovered, added to the jubilation of their special day.

No early photograph of the Methodist Chapel has yet been discovered, however the front has altered very little since it was built. The shaded stones contain the names of people who donated to the building fund.

It was at the end of November 1911 when one of the founder members of the Primitive Methodist chapel in Forest Town left the village for America. Joseph Share and his family departed for New York from where they would first travel 2000 miles to attend a Methodist Conference in Sioux City, Iowa. Following this they planned to take up ministerial work in the district of Algona.

Joseph Share

After the Sunday service in which Joseph Share preached his farewell sermon, a special meeting took place the next day when friends and colleagues paid their tributes to Mr & Mrs Share and presented them with gifts.[9]

A few years later in August 1920, Rev Share and his wife made a return visit to Forest Town and once again, Joseph Share preached at the chapel. They were warmly welcomed by the people of the village who again presented them with gifts to take back to their home in Newell, Iowa, U.S.A.[10]

The Forest Town Primitive Methodist chapel was not licensed for marriages[11] and did not have a burial ground. Marriages and burials would have taken place either at another Methodist church within the circuit, or possibly the Parish Church i.e. St Edmund's, Mansfield Woodhouse (or later St Alban's). Baptisms however did take place and the Baptism Register for the Forest Town Chapel commenced on 30th May 1909. From then until the end of that same year there were just five baptisms.

Baptised	***Born***	***Childs' Name***	***Parents***	***Surname***	***Abode***	***Occupation***	***Preacher***
30/ 5/1909	16/4/1909	Arthur	Woodhall & Edith	PARR	Forest Town	Coal Miner	Mr Fletcher
1909	1//8/1909	Dorothy	James Edward &Ellen Louise	SENIOR	Forest Town	Clerk	Mr Murray
8/ 8/1909	27/6/1909	Doris	Albert & Nellie	MILLERSHIP	Forest Town	Coal Miner	S Rowley
27/ 9/1909	28/8/1909	Joyce Mavis	Walter& Sarah Ann	HOBSON	Forest Town	Coal Miner	G Redram
31/10/1909	28/9/1909	Charles Ambrose	Alfred& Elizabeth Florence	MACE	23 Sixth Avenue	Coal Miner	F Hardy

A page from the Baptism Register.
Note only the year was entered for Dorothy Senior

In the years that followed many more baptisms took place and the register reveals local surnames such as, Moxon, Parker, Frost, Green, Cupit, Boden, Cutts, and many more. The occupation of the father is given and not surprisingly in this new village many of them were miners. Other occupations reveal:

Engine Winder - *Frank Pearson*, Blacksmith - *James Watson*
Screen______ - *John Cupit*, Railway Porter - *Albert Roper*
Assistant Under Manager - *Frederick Davis.*

The register also reveals a sign of the times when the occupation of *Joseph Smith*, *Luther Millard*, and *Thomas Rupert Taylor* are given as soldier.[12]

Over the following years, many events were held at the Primitive Methodist chapel. There were Sunday School Anniversaries in May, and parades around the village when a street collection was taken. Prize givings, parties, teas, and sales of provisions. These were all an important part of life in the village.

Surviving Sunday School accounts reveal the purchase of 300 Star Cards (attendance cards) in February 1910, two Star Registers and Sunday School Reports. The children who attended Sunday School were proud to have their star card stamped and looked forward to the prize giving event.

5

1910		Income	£	s	d
Jan	1	Balance in Hand	9	8	3½
"	2	8 School Hymn Books		3	0
"	9	2 " "			9
"	9	3 " "		1	1½
"	16	3 " "		1	1½
March		12 " "		4	6
		7 " "		2	7½
April	3rd	Collection		9	5½
May	22	En route Collection	2	10	9
"	"	Afternoon	3	2	0
"		Evening	4	12	3½
"	29	En route		18	11
	"	Afternoon	2	1	1
	"	Evening	4	0	6
	"	Donation		2	6
	"	Childrens Cards		14	4
May	16	proceeds from tea		9	8
		Income	29	2	11
		Expenditure	25	1	0
		Balance	4	1	11

Audited Found Correct
[illegible]
Jan 8/1911

6

1910		Expenditure	£	s	d
Jany		Connexional fund		3	-
		District Band of Hope fund		1	-
Feby	8	300 Star Cds at [illegible]		9	-
"	"	2 boxes of Stamps at 1/11		3	10
"	"	2 Star Registers @ 1/6		3	-
"	"	3 doz S S Hymnals 4½d		13	6
	"	S. School Reports		1	2
	"	Scholars Letters		4	
March	27	200 Labels @ 1/6 & Postage		3	3
	"	Carriage for Prizes			6
"	16	For. Cent. Tea		2	6
	22	Wreath for J. Ericson		13	0
May	16	540 Buns & pastry		16	9
	"	Sweet Cake		11	3
	"	White Bread		4	3
	"	Brown Bread		4	10½
	"	Tea Cakes & Milk		9	3½
	"	Paid to Caretaker		2	0
	"	Assundries			3
	"	Nuts & Sweets	1	2	6
		Butter Tea & Sugar	1	1	10
June	2nd	Scholars rewards	4	19	1
	"	3 doz Bibles & 2 doz Test	2	4	0
	6	"Centenary fund	6	0	0
	29	Music for Sermons	2	1	3
		Carriage for Bibles			6
		Presentation for Mr Slack		10	
April	29	To Mr Lee 1000 Hym Sheets	1	5	0
		25 Crown Bills		4	0
		6 Scripture Handbooks		1	1
		Expences for Scripture Exam		5	4
			25	1	0

Account showing top right, 300 star cards and 2 star registers

The accounts were meticulously kept over the years, a Caretakers fee is often paid but there is no indication of who this was. Many names do appear in the accounts such as those in the 1921 account; Mrs Heath, Mrs Carter, Mrs Turton, Mrs Hilton, Mrs Hoggets, Mrs Moxon, Mrs Hursthouse and Mr Wainman, the latter supplying 400 buns.

May	3rd	Sunday School Addmission Bo[illegible]	5	—	3	6
"	26th	Sweets for S.S. Treat	6	1	15	-
"	30th	Sunday School Rent (Mr. Gellott)	7	5	—	-
"	30th	Milk for S.S. Treat.	8	—	4	8
"	30th	Provisions from Marsden's. S.S. Treat	9	1	15	5
"	30th	Nuts for. S.S. Treat.	10	—	17	4
"	31st	Mrs Heath for bread.	11	—	4	5
"	31st	Mrs Carter for bread & cake.	12	—	7	-
"	31st	Mrs Turton for tea cakes.	13	—	4	5½
"	31st	Mrs Hilton for cake	14	—	6	-
"	31st	Mrs Hoggetts for cake	15	—	7	10½
"	31st	Mrs Moxon for tea-cakes	16	—	6	1
"	31st	Mrs Hursthouse for barm bread	17	—	6	9
"	31st	Mr Wainman for 400 buns	18	1	6	8

Expenditure for May 1921

The 1921 accounts also quote the cost of 120 scholars letters, giving an indication of how many young people were attending the chapel. They also give an insight into what everyone ate at the Sunday School treat. In December that year the cost of 150 scholars letters are listed as four shillings and sixpence (22½p), which gives an indication of how many more young people were attending this little chapel.[13]

From 1905 to 1921 the village had expanded greatly and had been through the troubled times of the war years. The building of the Primitive Methodist chapel had proved an important asset to the community of Forest Town. One hundred years on, in 2005, both the building and the worshippers have stood the test of time. It is still a lively and happy place.

The Wesleyan Chapel

In the village of Forest Town, the Methodist faith had many followers, some were Primitive Methodists who went to their chapel on Clipstone Road. There were however Methodists among the local community who preferred the Wesleyan traditions, and while it is unknown where they met in the early years of the village, from June 1909 their services were held in the newly opened Drill Hall.

It was on a Wednesday early in June that a special service was held to inaugurate the use of the Drill Hall for this purpose. Rev W. H. H. Kelshaw of Halifax Place Mission, Nottingham visited Forest Town for the occasion and in the afternoon he preached to a 'fairly decent congregation.' Appropriate to the occasion, a public tea and meeting followed. John Plowright Houfton, general manager of the Bolsover Colliery and a follower of the Wesleyans, presided over the meeting. Rev W. H. H. Kelshaw, Rev J. Wright (superintendent of the Mansfield Circuit), and Mr J. Simpson-Alcock were also on the platform of speakers. Mr Houfton said he was encouraged by the enthusiasm of those present to establish the Wesleyan faith in Forest Town. They also wanted their own chapel and were told that, 'with his characteristic generosity the Duke of Portland had given practically without charge, a suitable site for the chapel'.[14]

The Drill Hall where the first Wesleyan Methodist services were held

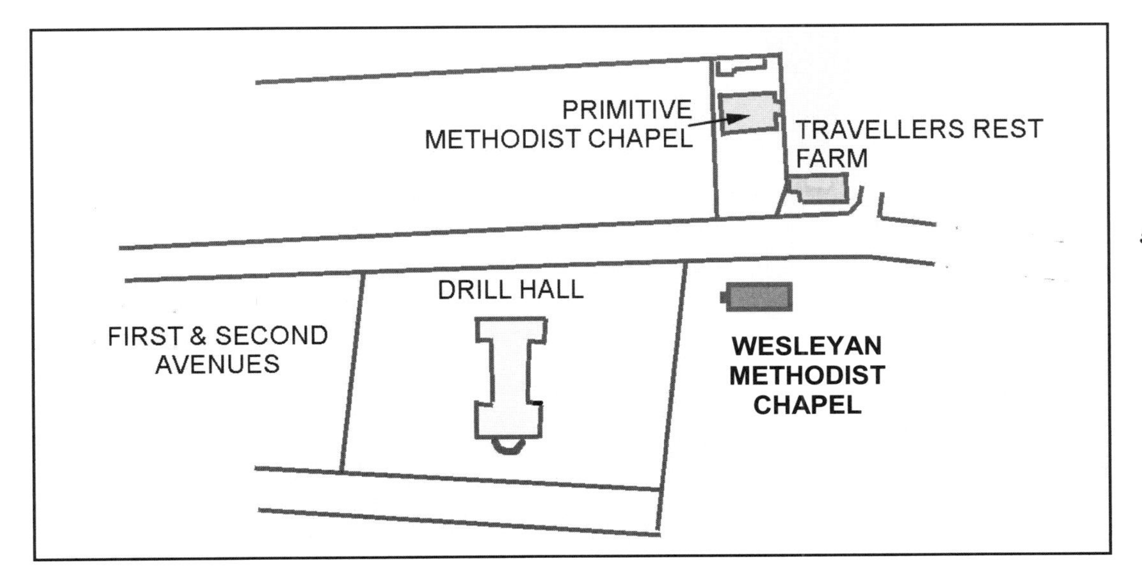

Plan showing the site of The Wesleyan Chapel

Despite that promise in June 1909 of land for the new chapel, the Wesleyan Methodists do not appear to have started a building fund until November 1910. The secretary was C. T. Beazley who lived on Second Avenue. A surviving Committee Book contains the names of local people who it can be assumed were contributing to the building fund and had a specific interest in the Wesleyan Chapel.[15]

Mr Parr			
Frank Butcher**	Ninth Avenue	_William Betts*_	Clipstone Road
William Keeton	Third Avenue	_Alec Reggin**_	
Tom Butcher*	Ninth Avenue	_T. Ward*_	Third Avenue
J. Francis Lee**	Clipstone Road	_Arthur Clark_	16 Third Avenue
Ethel Banner	8 Fifth Avenue	_May Bullock_	12 Fifth Avenue
Frank Staton	12 Fifth Avenue	_C. T. Beazley_	
Mr Egglestone		_Saml Banner**_	Barn Lane
Mr T. Lakin	George Street	_Mr Hy. Green**_	Ninth Avenue
Archie Green**		_W. Laykin*_	George Street
Reginald Blood	16 Sixth Avenue	_Dorothy Walker_	38 Clipstone Rd
Violet Smith	32 Ninth Avenue	_Annie Goodman_	
Tacey Watson**	20 Fifth Avenue	_Myles Butcher_	

Some are dated 1910* others 1911**
Some do not have an address

The Wesleyan chapel was eventually erected on land across the road from the Primitive Methodist chapel, (the site where St Patrick's Catholic church now stands). This was a wood and iron building which opened in May 1913 and is still referred to by many people as 'the tin chapel.'

The Wesleyan Chapel

It was 1910 when the Wesleyan baptism register for Forest Town started, and three baptisms were recorded. It has to be assumed these took place in the Drill Hall.

Baptised	*Childs Name*	*Parents*	*Surname*	*Abode*	*Born*	*Minister*
15.5.1910	Lina	Cornelius & Mary Ann	TURNER	26 Cambridge St Mansfield	9.4.1910	C.O. Oivers
30.5.1910	Edna Mary	Alfred & Harriett	KEMPIN	1. Eighth Ave	25.4.1910	J. Wright
14.8.1910	Bernard Jackson	Samuel & Mary Jane	BANNER	11. Big Barn Lane	22.7.1910	R.H. Williams

The three baptisms in 1910

Baptisms at both the Wesleyan and Primitive Methodist chapels were not frequent events, sometimes there was only one or two baptisms a year. When they did take place, the baptisms would no doubt have been a time of great joy for the Methodist congregations.[16]

The baptism registers for the two Methodists churches differ in as much that the Wesleyan register does not record the father's occupation. The information recorded does once again give names and addresses of local families, and many were from the Avenues. An example, taken from each year reveals the surnames:

1911	Beazley	2 Second Avenue
1913	Cupit	19 Fifth Avenue
1914	Keeton	31 Third Avenue
1915	Banner	26 Second Avenue
1916	Clement	Second Avenue
1917	Elliott	16 Eighth Avenue
1918	Bowyer	27 Second Avenue
1919		*No entries recorded*
1920	Marsh	16 Fourth Avenue
1921	Stennett	28 Seventh Avenue

As with the other churches in Forest Town, many services and other activities took place in the Wesleyan building; concerts, sales of work, and the harvest festivals would have been joyful community occasions. During the First World War years, special social events were held for soldiers from Clipstone Camp. Like the rest of the community, members of the Wesleyan Methodists were keen to do what they could for the soldiers whose fate was unknown. The account books not only give an insight into events held by the Wesleyans, but also where provisions were purchased; Oslers, Co-op, Mawers, Willoughby, Taylor, Middleton, Liptons and Cowpe (milk), these are recognisable as local shopkeepers or even farmers.[17]

It is interesting to note that on more than one occasion the expense of a loan of a piano is recorded. On one such occasion (the specific event is not recorded), the following is listed:[18]

Caretaker	3s	0d
Postage		6½
Lads Helping Caretaker		4
Piano	2	6
	6	4½

No doubt the lads helping the caretaker would have been happy to share the four pennies.

The old 'tin chapel,' its services and activities are still well remembered by many people in Forest Town today. However the numbers of those attending the chapel gradually declined, and it was obviously not feasible to continue holding services there. The chapel eventually closed in 1955, and the chapel and land were sold in 1956.[19]

NOTES

1 Oral history from a descendant of Joseph Share.
2 Mansfield & North Notts Reporter 31 March 1905.
3 Memorandum of appointment of New Trustees 5th December 1914. (In possession of Methodist Circuit Minister).
4 Mansfield & North Notts Advertiser 31 March 1905.
5 As above.
6 Oral history.
7 Mansfield & North Notts Advertiser 2 June 1905.
8 This lady was related to Albert William Smith, one of the trustees of the new building.
9 Forest Town History Collection, in private hands.
10 Mansfield & North Notts Advertiser 13 August 1920. Joseph Share wrote a book Firelight Flashes, published 1937 USA - a copy was sent to relatives in Nottinghamshire.
11 The Primitive Chapel was eventually licensed for marriages in 2001.
12 Baptism Register in possession of Methodist Circuit Minister.
13 Primitive Methodist Account Book 1908 -1943 with the Chapel.
14 Mansfield & North Notts Advertiser 11 June 1909.
15 NA NC/MR9/122/1.
16 Baptism Register in possession of Methodist Circuit Minister.
17 NA NC/MR9/122/1, (Cowpe may have been from Newlands Farm).
18 NA NC/MR9/112/51.
19 As above.

12 - THE VILLAGE SCHOOL

As gradually more miners with young families moved into the houses that were being built in the new village of Forest Town, the question of where to educate the children soon became a necessary consideration by the respective authorities. The first children to live in the village were said to have been taken on farm, or coal carts to schools some distance away in Mansfield. It is recalled that some children went to St Lawrence's, or Newgate Lane schools.[1]

This however could only be a temporary arrangement, for as the village population grew, and the number of children increased, it soon became a topic of some discussion and concern.

> 5th February 1904 *Children from the colliery village near Crown Farm are overcrowding Mansfield schools and the County Council is to be reminded of its responsibility for the provision of school accommodation at Mansfield Woodhouse, (the new village came under Mansfield Woodhouse).*[2]

Forest Town urgently needed a school of its own, and local councils were in favour of using the new Primitive Methodist schoolroom,[3] or the new mission church.[4] The Nottingham County Council Education Committee rejected the idea, they believed the initial responsibility for providing an education for the Forest Town children lay with them.[5]

Temporary schools to accommodate 120 children were considered in June 1904,[6] and by December 1904 it had been decided to provide a school for 300 children.[7]

A loan of £150 was requested from the Local Government Board to purchase a half-acre site from the Duke of Portland. The cost was one shilling a yard. [sic][8] J. Greenwood of Mansfield were to do the foundations[9] and in September 1905 a temporary iron building was purchased from Ginger Lee & Co of Manchester.[10] The necessary work was started and in March 1906 the name of the school was decided as:

'The Mansfield Woodhouse New Sherwood Temporary Council School'.[11]

The Initial Cost of the School [12]

Provision of the Site	£150
Erection of Iron Building	£600
Erection of Fencing	£151
Furniture and Fixings	£124

Staff for the school were employed, including the headmaster Mr Rudge who was appointed at a salary of £150 per year, and the building was ready for its first pupils. The first entry in the school logbook stated:[13]

5 March 1906

The School (Mixed and Infants Depts.) was opened today under the Headmastership of Mr William Warren Rudge late principle assistant of Mansfield Woodhouse Council School, with 94 children on the books. During the morning the school was visited by C. J. Bristowe Esq. Director of Education

Staff

Mr Wm. Rudge. Head Teacher – First Class Trained Certificated Master (Kings' Coll. Lond.)

Miss Florence Allen Bodell - Certificated Assistant in charge of the Infants.

Mrs Kate Evelyn Rudge - Uncertificated Mistress in the Mixed Dept.

Miss Adeline Frost - Supplementary Teacher in the Mixed Dept.

Among the first pupils recorded in the Admission Registers[14] some of the oldest were:

NAME	BORN	PARENT/GUARDIAN	ADDRESS
Hilda Mary YOUNG	1891	Francis	9 Sixth Avenue
John David FOX	1892	George	11 Fourth Avenue
George William PERRY	1893	Mark	5 Fifth Avenue
William KITCHEN	1893	William Wigman	16 Fourth Avenue
Gertrude WINTER	1893	Arthur	21 Second Avenue
William HINTON	1893	John William	First Avenue
Arthur SWAIN	1894	Thomas	7 Sixth Avenue
George CUTTS	1894	William	4 Sixth Avenue
Edward Wall WEBSTER	1894	John William	28 Eighth Avenue
Thomas MURDEN	1895	John	14 Fourth Avenue
Ethel ANNABLE	1895	Frederick	31 Eighth Avenue

Children from the two local farms were also able to attend this new school. Arthur Vincent from the Travellers Rest, and Leonard Newton from Crown Farm are listed among the first pupils.

In September 1906, two high chairs for teachers were received, it is easy to visualise how the female teachers would have looked as they sat on those two high chairs in their long skirts. The rows of children who sat in front of them knew they were there to learn, and they knew they had to behave. In those early months on a dull day, it is presumed that the classrooms were quite gloomy, for in November the school logbook states, 'lamps for lighting the school arrived'. These must have been a very welcome addition to the school.

By December 1906 the number of pupils had more than doubled; the school now had 219 pupils. The school curriculum was established and included lessons on:

Health, Moral Instruction, Courtesy,
Thrift, Patriotism, Home Life.

From the onset the school was visited frequently by both school managers and inspectors, and children were regularly examined in religious instruction, a subject that included;

Repetition of the scriptures
Singing from memory
Knowledge of the Old Testament
Knowledge of the New Testament

Just less than a year after it opened the school was making new provisions. On the 28 February 1907, it was recorded in the logbook 'The schools close tomorrow (Friday) owing to removal of furniture to new infant room and to allow staff to get settled into new rooms'.[15] It has to be assumed that this room was still in the same temporary iron building and that in some way the building was being reorganised.

In May, fifteen desks were received for the school followed by a further supply of twenty-two duel desks in September, desks that were supplied from the Bennet Furnishing Co, in Glasgow. An entry in the logbook makes us aware that the Forest Town school children were sat at combined desks and seats as this stated 'the seat casting of one of the new desks supplied by Bennet's was broken in transit'. Further supplies of furniture and other items were received over the following months, these included two new doormats which arrived on 25 October 1907 'to take the place of those worn out.'[16]

On the 10 August 1908 the school restarted after the summer holidays with the mention of two new members of staff, Mr Robert Lee, and Mrs Naomi Rothwell nee Bradbury, they were to work in the Mixed Division of the school. The logbook also records:

The children reassembled this morning but to enable the teachers to move the stock into the new school they were dismissed and work commences tomorrow morning, 11th August.

No doubt the children were delighted to find they had an additional holiday. It is not clear from plans and documentation just what building was being referred to as the new school.

The whole school until August 1909 was under one headmaster, Mr Rudge. However with a growing school, this was set to change, and the Mixed Dept logbook on 9th August 1909 records;

> *'The Infant School now forms a separate department.' The senior school now had six classes with the following teachers*:
>
> *Mr Rudge, Mr Walker, Miss Carr, Mr Lee,*
> *Mr Townsend, Mrs Rothwell, Mr Ward.*

The new Infants Department now had a headmistress, Miss Mabel Silverton Stafford and three other members of staff, Ethel North, Dorothy Warner and Elizabeth Shooter. The school inspectors, who had been concerned at the staffing arrangements on their last visit in June, welcomed the instigation of the infants as a separate department.[17]

Miss Stafford and children

Children moved from the Infants to the Mixed Department and stayed there until they were of school leaving age. They then required an exemption certificate that allowed them to leave school and start work. Some children were clever enough to obtain a scholarship enabling them to transfer to the Grammar School. However this was very much dependant on the financial situation of their parents and a number of children had to forgo the opportunity of further education and to start work instead.

School holidays are well recorded in the logbooks. Empire Day was always an event, lessons about the Empire were taught in the morning and the children were then given the afternoon off. Holidays on Shrove Tuesday, Whitsuntide, and Mansfield Woodhouse Feast holiday in July were other memorable events in the school year. National celebrations also gave the opportunity for extra holidays, such as on the 16th June 1911, when the school closed for a weeks holiday in honour of the Coronation of his Majesty King George the Fifth. The children were possibly just as excited to learn they had extra holidays as to hear about the coronation.

Life at the school could be extra difficult at times as illness often prevailed among both the children, and the staff. Measles, whooping cough and chickenpox, were common illnesses of that time and often resulted in epidemics in the village such as those in November 1907, and March 1911 (measles), December 1913 (chickenpox). There were times when illness resulted in the school being closed;

24 February 1915 - Closure under article 57, at the end of morning session. Measles Epidemic.[18]

It was the 15th March before the school reopened.

The school staff were often recorded as being absent because of illness such as influenza or neuralgia, or occasionally there were incidents like the one in May 1908, 'Mr T.A. Townsend was absent from school owing to an accident to his bicycle!' [19]

Events relating to the staff, which are mentioned in the logbooks, give an awareness of both personal and national events.

25th February 1908 - *Mr W. T. Gamble has obtained a day's leave of absence in order to attend a relative's funeral today.* Three days later the entry reads *Mr W. T. Gamble's engagement as an uncertificated teacher terminated today. His parents are leaving the district.*

3rd April 1911 *The headmaster was absent from school for most of the day to enable him to collect the census schedules in his district.*

4th September 1912 *Mrs Whiteoak is absent from school today as her son is undergoing an operation.*

11th June 1913 *Mr T. A. Townsend has obtained leave of absence for today in order to be married, the head teacher has charge of his class.*

5th March 1917 *Mrs Titchener was absent from school today (Monday) as her husband was on leave.*

18th October 1918 *Mrs Morley has sent a message to the effect that she will not be able to attend school as her husband who is a soldier is coming home on leave.*

Throughout the early years there were many teachers at the school, these included: Mr and Mrs Rudge, the Misses Stafford, Sarll, Poole, Bodell, Shooter Frost, Swain, Elliott, Mrs Whiteoak and Titchener. Among the male teachers were Mr Lee, Smith, Harrison and Townsend. There were many others, some who were fully qualified (certificated), and others who were not (uncertificated). While some teachers were with the school many years, others were only there for a very short time.

Mr Rudge with children 1910

Very little is known about the school caretakers; in 1906 the County Education minutes recorded Mrs Cousins as being employed with a yearly salary of £19.10.00d (£19.50).[20] The school logbook however records on 14th September 1908 that Mr A Jepson caretaker of the school died on Saturday morning Sept 12th, it also notes that Mr Watson of Clipstone Road has been appointed to succeed him. There was obviously no delay in obtaining a new caretaker for the school.[21]

The work in the school progressed with regular visits by his Majesty's inspectors who were both critical and complimentary in their reports.[22]

> September 1907 *The Infants Department was good considering the rapid growth of the school*
>
> October 1908 *The Infants' Department is at a disadvantage through all the children being in one room*
>
> April 1915 *The head teacher conducts the school in an energetic and efficient way*
>
> September 1920 *In visiting the classes we were pleased to find that several of the teachers can teach scripture so as to emphasise its religious value*

School managers such as Mr Bull, Mr Robinson, Mr Bingley, Mr Beeton and Margaret Bull regularly checked the registers. The school nurse also visited the school to check the children's hair. On 18th January 1910 when she visited the school and examined the hair of the girls – eleven were excluded for two days. [23]

FOREST TOWN PUPILS AND THEIR WORK

Nellie Hargreaves
was born on the 21st October 1900

She started Forest Town School in
October 1907 after her family moved
from Warsop Vale to live
in Second Avenue.

In 1914 she received a
Certificate of Merit in an essay
competition.

She left school on the 13th March 1914

NATURE NOTE BOOK
Name Nina Gittings.
SISSON & PARKER, NOTTINGHAM.

Nina Gittings
lived at 13 First Avenue
and started Forest Town School on the 19th May 1913
when she was 5 years old.

She left school on the 22nd July 1921
to start work aged 13.

These pages are from one of her school work books.
They show that she enjoyed nature lessons.

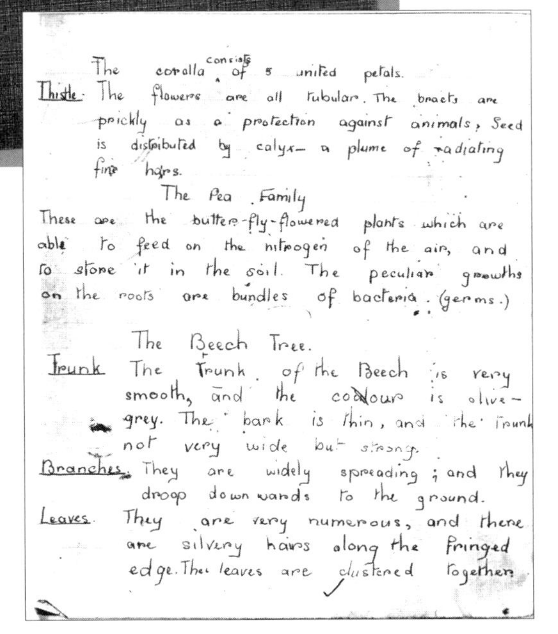

The corolla consists of 5 united petals.

Thistle. The flowers are all tubular. The bracts are prickly as a protection against animals, Seed is distributed by calyx— a plume of radiating fine hairs.

The Pea Family

These are the butter-fly-flowered plants which are able to feed on the nitrogen of the air, and to store it in the soil. The peculiar growths on the roots are bundles of bacteria. (germs.)

The Beech Tree.

Trunk. The trunk of the Beech is very smooth, and the colour is olive-grey. The bark is thin, and the trunk not very wide but strong.

Branches. They are widely spreading; and they droop downwards to the ground.

Leaves. They are very numerous, and there are silvery hairs along the fringed edge. The leaves are clustered together.

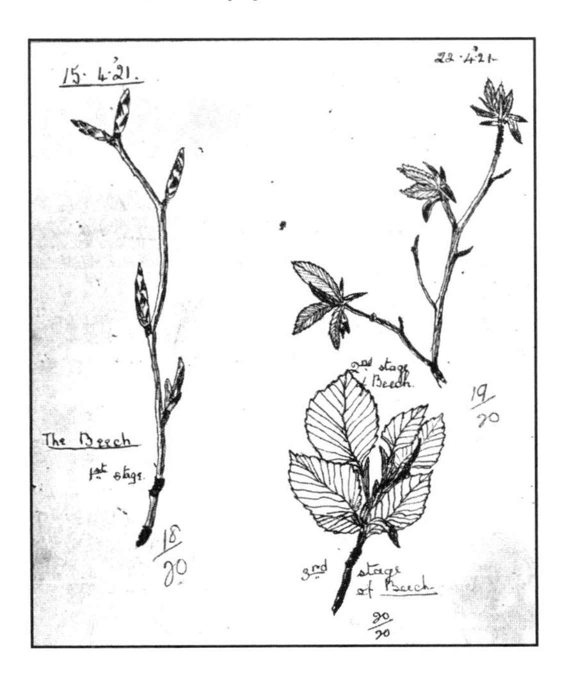

School lessons included drawing for the boys and needlework for the girls. Arrangements were made in January 1914 for thirty-six girls to attend York Street Council School, Mansfield Woodhouse to receive instruction in cookery.[24] This was to alternate each week with needlework as part of household management lessons. Children went on nature walks, learnt poetry, and took part in school plays.

As the number of children attending the school grew, both they and the teachers had to cope with overcrowding in what was referred to as temporary buildings. The Land Tax Records dated 23 June 1915 record the New Sherwood School, Forest Town as a

> *Site with permanent school, temporary iron buildings, temporary wooden buildings, and necessary outbuildings. All the buildings used for the purpose of a Public Elementary School.* Additional notes state, *A well-built brick & tile school. Large additions nearing completion at the time of inspection. Rather difficult to see exactly what portion was existing in 1909. Several W/CL [wood cladding] erections now used as classrooms, in very bad condition. Playground in bad condition owing to building operations.* [25]

An item headed Subsequent Expenditure gives the total cost of erection of permanent school, temporary iron buildings and wooden buildings as £6,000, which is an interesting comparison to the £600 stated for the erection of the first iron building in 1905.

The above entry and some early class photographs suggest that there was a brick building as early as 1913. However while the new permanent brick building would have been a great asset to the teaching facilities of the school, it does not receive any worthy recording in the logbooks, just one entry was found in the Infant School logbook;

> 18 October 1915
> *Re-opened school after Autumn Holiday at 9.00am in the permanent building.*

The school buildings whether temporary or permanent at Forest Town have always been an important part of life of the village. It was there that the local children received a good basic education, one that has stayed with them throughout their adult life. Fond memories of the teachers still prevail, despite the painful reprimands received by some pupils!

Today, (2005) the red brick permanent school with its various additions and alterations, is still an important centre for education. Many of the young children who pass through the doors know that their parents, grandparents, and great grandparents have also gone there before them. Each and everyone has their place in the history of this village school.

In the classroom 1913

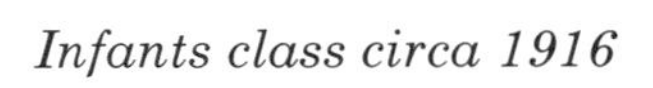

Infants class circa 1916

NOTES

1 Oral history - Mrs Cowley Mansfield 1994.
2 Mansfield & North Notts Advertiser 5 February 1904.
3 NA DC/MW 1/3/2/1.
4 NA CC3 12/9/1 Elementary Education Sub-Committee.
5 NA CC3/12/20/1 Sites & Building Committee March 1905.
6 NA CC3/12/20/1 Sites & Building Committee June 1904.
7 NA CC3 12/9/2 Elementary Education Sub-Committee December 1904.
8 As above.
9 NA CC3/12/2/3 Elementary Education Sub-Committee October 1905.
10 NA CC3/12/2/3 Elementary Education Sub-Committee September 1905.
11 NA CC3/12/2/3 Elementary Education Sub-Committee March 1906.
The name written at the front of the Log book in March 1906 reads 'New Sherwood Council School, Forest Town, Mansfield.'
12 NA CC3/12/2/3 Elementary Education Sub-Committee December 1905.
13 School Logbook (in Private Hands).
14 School Admission Registers (in Private Hands).
15 School Logbook (in Private Hands).
16 As above.
17 As above.
18 As above.
19 As above.
20 NA CC3/12/2/3 March 1906.
21 School Logbook (in Private Hands).
22 As above.
23 As above.
24 As above.
25 PRO IR 58/55343.

13 - THE VILLAGE SHOPS

No village would be complete without shops and the first shops in Forest Town are reputed to have been in the homes of people in the Avenues.[1] As the building of houses not shops would have been the immediate priority of the Bolsover Colliery Company, the first shops were no doubt established in this way to provide people with some basic provisions.

There is no official documentation to confirm this, and oral history has to be relied on. Various elderly people however have repeated the same story over the years, people who were among the first village children and whose families were some of the first inhabitants of the Avenues. They have often recollected that newspapers, sweets and other sundries were sold in the kitchens or front rooms of Avenue houses. Eventually when shops were built some of those early shopkeepers like Mrs Rawlins who had a sweet shop in her back kitchen on Ninth Avenue, moved to a 'proper shop' on Clipstone Road.[2]

While initially the 'front room' shops provided for some of their needs, the village people would have to travel on foot, or horse and cart to the shops in Mansfield Woodhouse or Mansfield, for other items. The Co-operative Society was a popular shopping facility of that time, and some of the first Forest Town inhabitants were members of the Co-operative Society well before Forest Town had a Co-op store of its own.

Septimus Swaby, Arthur Faulkner,
Robert & Sarah Silcock,
John Murden and Elizabeth Cheetham

are names that can be discovered in the Mansfield Co-operative Society Minute Books, as early as 1905; their address is just given as Forest Town.

In July 1905 the general manager of the Bolsover Colliery Company wrote to the Mansfield Co-operative Society requesting the establishing of a store in Forest Town. This was obviously considered favourably, for in September that year the Society were in contact with Mr Sykes (land owner), regarding the purchase of a plot of land for the new store.

There was some lengthy discussion over the price of the land as Mr Sykes was trying to obtain 10/- (50p) per yard for the land and the Co-operative Society felt this was too high. The eventual agreement was a price of 8/6d (42½p) a yard. Mr Sykes also agreed that he would not sell any other portions of his land for the erection of shops that would sell goods such as grocery, boots, drapery and butchering. This of course only applied to land that Mr Sykes owned, but it did show that the Co-op was obviously attempting to corner the market and avoid competition.

Fourteen quotations for building the new Co-op were received. They ranged from £760 to £547, and Vallance & Blythe who submitted the lowest quote won the contract. Additional to the price for the building there were various other costs such as

6 new counters for Drapery side £28
2 new fixtures, Grocery and Provisions £33

Eighteen months after his initial inquiry John Plowright Houfton, general manager of the Bolsover Colliery Company, officially opened the Forest Town Co-op in February 1907. J. G. Cawthorne was appointed as manager, and G. H. Sleigh was employed to work in the butchery department. The new shop had rules, as prior to the opening it was agreed that 'no credit be given at the new Forest Town Branch.' [3]

This Co-op was situated at the top of Main Avenue, and the windows originally faced on to Main Avenue. In later years after various extensions they were altered to face on to Clipstone Road.[4] As village people walked up the central avenue towards the main road (or High Street as it was sometimes referred to), they would pass the Co-op windows full of goods encouraging them to walk inside. Eight years after it first opened, the shop was extended and it has been altered in various ways since then.

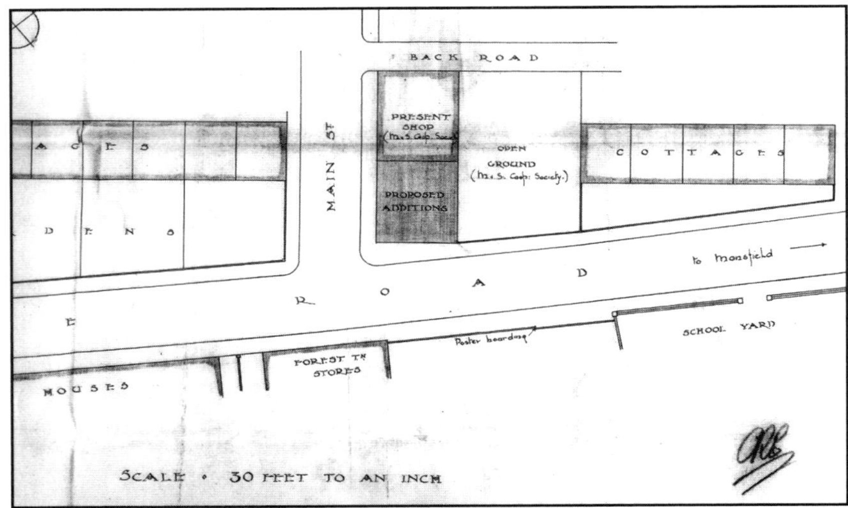

Plan showing original Co-op site and proposed additions in 1915 (From document in Nottinghamshire Archives DC/MW Co-op: Clipstone Rd 1915 Proposed additions to Mansfield & Sutton Co-op)

One young lady who worked in the drapery department, was Bertha Buxton. Bertha, born in 1901 lived in Second Avenue with her parents. She had previously attended Forest Town School and left there in 1914. Just how long she worked at the Forest Town Co-op is unknown.[5]

The Co-op of course did have local competition, for at the time the Co-op was being both planned and built, plans were also being drawn up for shops and houses on the main Clipstone Road (sometimes referred to as High Street). Once these were built the people of Forest Town were soon able to choose where they made their purchases.

The Co-op, looking down Main Avenue, note the delivery barrow.

Among these in February 1906, were a house and shop for Mr Kemp (next to where the Prince Charles Pub now stands). On the next plot to Mr Kemp's, a house and shop was to be erected for Mr Heath. By October 1906 a house and shop with a bay window above the shop was being planned for Mr Whiteoak.[6] These people may not have lived in the properties themselves, they could have rented them out to others or resold them.

Additional housing was also being planned on this top road (Clipstone Road), for Mr A. F. Houfton, (a block of four), Mr Hayes, Mr Lee, Mr Scott and Mr Dovey. Surviving plans and documents reveal that some of the properties were very roomy buildings, with good-sized cellars. Additionally some of the premises also had stables at the rear, these would have been essential as some traders hawked their wares around the local area with a horse and cart. A plaque over one of the shops can still be seen today on Clipstone Road and suggests that by 1907 both shops and houses must have been reasonably well developed.

By May 1907 Forest Town had a sub Post Office.[7] This was in one of three shops built near to the Methodist Church and the Post Office was the middle of the three shops, (next to where the Post Office is today in 2005). Shadrach Osler was the sub Postmaster[8] and he lived there with his wife Eliza and son Montague. Additional to postal facilities the shop sold a variety of things, including postcards and wallpaper.[9] It has been said that Shadrach Osler was one of the first people in Forest Town to own a car, which in the war years he used as a taxi.

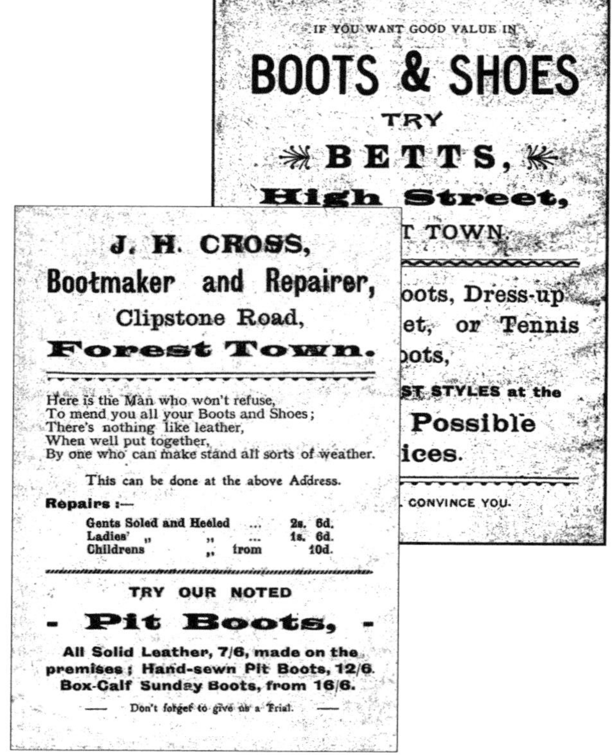

Additional to Shadrach Osler, other shopkeepers at that time were Kemp, Kitchener, Murden, Betts, and Gilway. These can be found listed in the 1908 Linney's Almanac,[10] and while their surnames and the word shopkeeper are given, unfortunately the type of shop they had is not listed. However advertisements in a 1909 Horticultural Society Catalogue do give an insight into the various shops at that time and what people in the village could purchase. Footwear could be purchased from Betts, or H. Cross who would also repair them. It is interesting to note that while both these shops are on the same road, Betts refer to it as the High Street, and Cross as Clipstone Road.

It was not just the footwear trade where there was competition in the village for with Gilway's Grocery & Provision Dealer and Winfield the Butcher, there would have been rivalry with the Co-operative Store just across the road from them.

Traders further afield were also keen to attract the custom of Forest Town people in 1909. An advertisement for the Carpenters Arms declared; *They were the Nearest House to Forest Town and it was where you could get Brampton Fine Ales and Stout, in sparkling condition.* While G. H. Oade's, of Church Street, Mansfield offered '*wise words*' *to both men and women of Forest Town about their tailor-made suits and costumes – their clothes were cut and tailor-made on the premises.*[11]

In 1910 the number of establishments for Forest Town listed in the Linney's Almanac had grown, and more information was given.[12]

The trade directories reveal that over the next few years while some shops changed hands, other shopkeepers remained and continued serving the people of Forest Town. In 1911 F. Whiteoak is recorded as the newsagent not W. J. Adams. By 1912 the barber is F. Arnold. This was a barber who earned himself the nickname of *Sweeny Todd*, for he was said to be always gazing outside as he worked and in doing so was apt to nip his customers ears when cutting their hair.

Shops on the 'High Street' (Clipstone Road). Forest Town 1910.

Shopkeeper	Trade
	Forest Town Stores
	Globe Tea Company
W. Morley	Barber
S. Winfield	Butcher
T. Gilway	Grocer & Cycle Stores
W. Betts	Boot & Shoe Dealer
Mrs Kitchener	Milliner, etc.
J. T. Goodman	Carter
F. Frith	Greengrocer
A. Ramsdale	Fish Shop
W.J. Adams	Newsagent
S. Osler	Post Office
A. Cross	Shoemaker

It was not uncommon for more than one trade to be done from the same shop. The post office sold a variety of things, Gilway (1910) was both grocer and cycle stores, and A. Ramsdale of the fish shop was also an omnibus proprietor, (see 1915 example right). He appears to have carried on both trades throughout the war years and well into the 1920's.

By 1922 house/shop numbers are given in the directory and give a clearer indication of which shop was where.[13] While the directory does list the occupiers of houses between the shops, only the shops are listed. [See chart page 72]

Shops on the Clipstone Road, Forest Town 1915

Shopkeeper	Trade
	Forest Town Stores
	Globe Tea Company
F. Arnold	Barber
S. Winfield	Butcher
T. Willoughby	General Dealer
T.Willoughby	Fish & Chips
Mrs Walker	Milliner etc.
J.T.Goodman	Carter
Lebeter	Greengrocer
A. Ramsdale	Fish Shop & Omnibus Proprietor
Mr Marriott	Newsagent
S. Osler	Post Office
A. Cross	Shoemaker

People walking up the main avenue could not fail to be aware of the large shop facing them from the top road, this was the Forest Town Stores. It is recalled as

a big shop, the full depth of the building. It had a beer counter, and sweets on one side, and cheese and bacon. In the back were big bins with scoops.[14]

Those were the days before pre-packed food when everything was measured out and wrapped, or groceries such as flour or sugar were scooped out of large bins, weighed and put into bags in the shop. The shop floor was wood and had sawdust on it.[15] The Forest Town Stores became a Beer Off within a short time of it opening. It was many years later in 1952, when it was converted into the Prince Charles Public House.

Forest Town Stores, other shops and houses on Clipstone Road. The photograph is taken from near the Co-op and the vehicle (possibly a charabanc) is parked on Main Avenue. Note the remains of an old boundary hedge.

1922 Shops on the left hand side of the Clipstone Road, Forest Town, going towards Clipstone

No	Shopkeeper	Trade
2	B. Middleton	Forest Town Stores
4		Taylors Stores
6	F. Arnold	Barber
8	S. Winfield	Butcher
10	Mrs Willoughby	General Dealer
12	W. Barnes	Druggist
14	Mrs Ranby	Milliner etc
16	J.T.Goodman	Carter
30	Lebeter	Confectioner
34	A. Ramsdale	Fish Shop & Omnibus Proprietor
44	Marriott	Newsagent
50	S. Osler	Post Office
52	A. Cross	Shoemaker

This photograph looking towards the crossroads shows Shadrach Osler and his son Montague in front of the Post Office. The letter box can be seen in the wall.

Despite various modifications to the shop fronts over the years, renumbering of the properties, and the Forest Town Stores being converted, it is still possible to identify all of the original shops today, most are still in use. Many elderly people who have lived most of their lives in Forest Town still reminisce about the early shops and the people who had them:

> *Lebeters had a sweet shop on the corner, she was a nice person, she had high necks [her dress] with a lace collar and we used to go up the steps for sweets.*[16]

> Oslers had the post office. The only telephone was in the post office. The post box was on the outside wall and was emptied from inside the shop.[17]

Additionally people also recall that a petrol pump once stood outside the post office, this may have been because Shadrach Osler owned a car and also ran a taxi service in later years.

While records are essential tools in local history, it is memories such as these that help us to go back in time, and visualise the shops as they really were when the high street was the shopping precinct for the village of Forest Town.

NOTES

1 Oral history various people.
2 Oral history Mr & Mrs Haslam, Ninth Avenue 1992.
3 NA DDGN14/1/1/3.
4 The bricked up windows can still be seen on Main Avenue.
5 Bertha Buxton born 1901, daughter of Amos and Annie (nee Glazzard) Buxton lived in Second Avenue, known to have lived in Forest Town from 1909. Information from Ken Ward, (grandson), Australia and School Registers.
6 NA DC/MW.
7 NA DC/MW 1/3/2/1-3.
8 BPMA. Postmaster Generals Minutes Books No 25909.
9 Oral history Mr & Mrs D Osler 1994 (grandson of Shadrach Osler).
10 Linneys Almanac was published yearly and are to be found in Mansfield Local Studies Library.
11 Horticultural Exhibition Brochure 1909 – copy in Private Hands.
12 Copies of Linneys Almanac can be found in Mansfield Local Studies Library.
13 In later years all the property numbers were changed.
14 Oral history Mr & Mrs Billings 1992.
(Mrs Billings parents, the Bennets lived at the Forest Town Stores.)
15 As above.
16 Oral history Dolly Clarke 1992.
17 Oral history Mr & Mrs E Morris 1992.

14 - THE INSTITUTE

Today, when the working day is over we have the television to watch, the radio to listen to, music to play, or numerous other leisure facilities to follow. Life however has not always been like this, especially for the working man. The men who first worked at Mansfield (Crown Farm) Colliery, worked long hours, and the work was dirty and strenuous. They walked home in their pit muck, for there was no pithead baths until 1936. After eating, and no doubt sleeping, depending on their shifts, some would take the opportunity to work in their allotments, practice with the colliery band or have a drink at the 'club'.

Providing a Miners' Institute (club) in each of its villages, was an early priority of the Bolsover Colliery Company. They believed it was important to establish a place where the men could enjoy both leisure and social facilities, including somewhere they could partake of moderate liquid refreshment. While the Company did have the men's welfare at heart, they also believed that by both providing and encouraging the workforce to use facilities in their own village, this would result in a better attendance at work. It was indirectly a way of controlling them.

The Bolsover Colliery Company's [BCC] Miners' Institutes had rules, which indirectly meant the company had some kind of control over their workforce. It was known that the majority of miners enjoyed a drink. This would help to wash the coal dust from their lungs, and for most men this meant going to the club. If it is surmised that the same rules applied at all the BCC Miners' Institutes, then the Mansfield miners were aware that:

No member may be supplied with more than two glasses of intoxicating liquor between 10am and 6pm, nor more than three glasses between 6pm and 10pm.[1]

Providing club facilities was an early priority when the Mansfield Colliery and Forest Town were being developed. In June 1905 just after coal had been reached at the new colliery, the Derbyshire Times newspaper featured a very long article headed:

The Bolsover Company's Latest Enterprise

The article tells of the new Mansfield Colliery, and how the associated village of Forest Town was developing and includes:

The sinking has meant the employment of about 200 men who have resided there, and for their recreation a temporary club has been erected, but will by and by give way to a permanent place. [2]

The article does not say where the club was, and as very few documents on the building of the village have survived, this has not been officially established. However, oral history decrees that the first club [3] was in two houses on Fifth Avenue, and there is no reason to dispute this. Both the knowledge of drinking premises and drinking stories are well remembered by many village residents.[4]

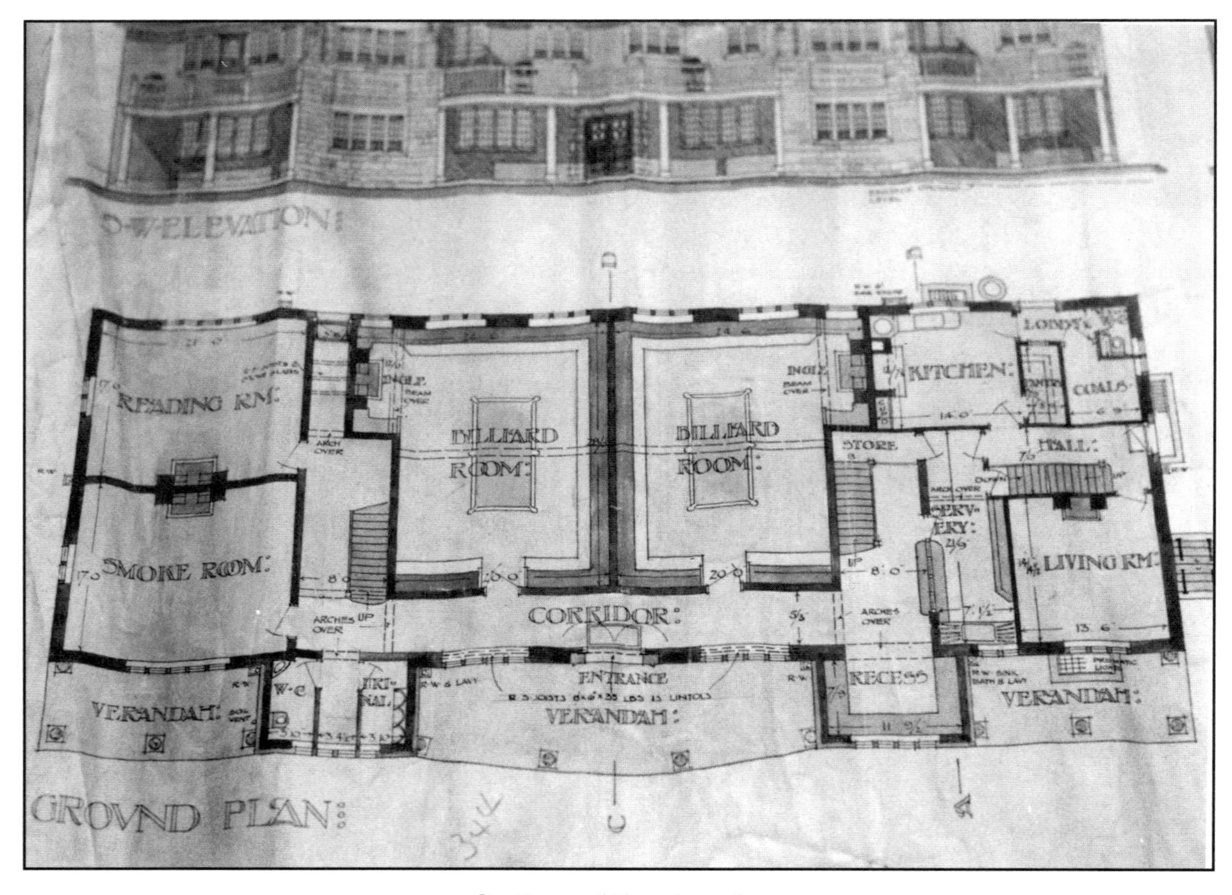

Sections of the plans for
The proposed Workmen's Institute Forest Town for The Bolsover Colliery Co Ltd
Percy F Houfton Architect Chesterfield September 1906.
(Original document in Nottinghamshire Archives DC/MW 3/9/10/1).

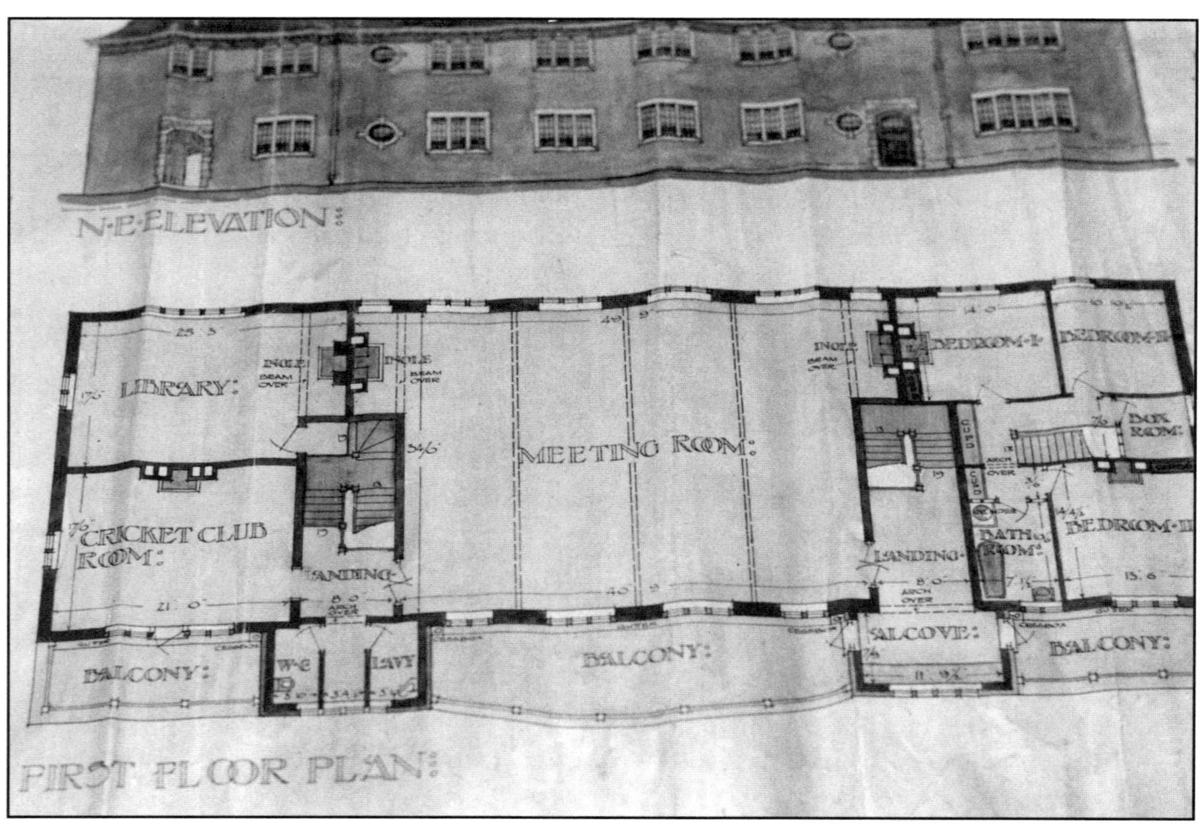

In 1906 permanent premises were being considered and Chesterfield Architect Percy Bond Houfton, produced plans for a Workman's Institute at Forest Town. These colourful plans drawn on linen can be seen in the Nottinghamshire Archives.[5]

Nothing is known of the actual building process, when the work started, or how long this took. The builder was H. Oakey of Bolsover, and the official opening of the splendid new building took place on the evening of Wednesday the 8th April 1908.[6]

However newspaper reports suggest that both the building and the grounds may have been in use well before this date;

> 16th August 1907 *The Second annual exhibition of flowers and garden produce was held on the Forest Town Cricket Ground.*[7]
>
> 13th September 1907 *Members of the Workmens Club had their first annual trip on Saturday. Seventy left the Institute at 8:30am in charabancs, reaching Matlock about noon.*[8]

In April 1908 when the new Forest Town Institute was formally opened there were already 250 members. The impressive Institute which cost £5,000 to build and furnish, was said to have larger and better facilities than those at Bolsover and Creswell, the two other mining villages built by the Bolsover Colliery Company.

The Forest Town Miners' Institute

Once again, the opening ceremony of a new building in the Forest Town mining village was a notable event, and warranted lengthy reports in the local newspapers. These provide an excellent description of both the building, and the grounds that were established in an area covering seventeen acres. The building of brick with stone dressing was erected close to the Clipstone Road. While local people refer to that as the back, and the front as facing the sports field, the Mansfield Reporter newspaper stated at the rear of the building was a large balcony, with extensive views.

> *The view from here in the summer will be extremely interesting, for the members will be able to look out upon the grounds, now rough common land but which is being transformed into a cricket pitch, bowling green, two tennis courts and a cinder track which will encircle the cricket pitch. Immediately in front of the Institute will be gardens, and numerous flowering trees and shrubs will be planted. In one corner of the grounds will be greenhouses and there will also be a cricket pavilion. It is estimated that the total cost of laying out the grounds will be £2.000.*[9]

Inside, the building on the ground floor was:

Two billiard rooms, each containing a full-sized table.
A spacious smoke room, and other smaller rooms.
A bar with seating accommodation in a recess.

Upstairs:

There was a large concert hall, which could accommodate over 350 people.
A comfortable library and a reading room.
A committee room.

An apartment was also provided for a caretaker.

In each room, there was a large open, old-fashioned fireplace, with seats on either side. Throughout the building the woodwork and the chairs were of oak, which added to the splendour of the interior.

Oswald Bainbridge (jun.) opened the new Institute. It had been anticipated that Emerson Bainbridge, owner of the Bolsover Colliery Company would have performed this honour, however as he was delayed in the South of France it was left to his son to officially declare the Institute open. In doing so Oswald Bainbridge congratulated the members on

> *At last having come into possession of the premises he added that he hoped the men would take full advantage of the new premises and facilities, as the old place was quite inadequate for their requirements.* [10]

He was no doubt referring to the rooms in the two houses on Fifth Avenue. A vote of thanks was given to Mr Bainbridge by the colliery manager, Mr Bingley and seconded by Mr Davis.

John P. Houfton who chaired the opening ceremony spoke of the progress of the

Bolsover Colliery Company, of the number of men and boys they employed, and the vast amount of coal that was being produced. He said:

> *That the company recognised its responsibilities and obligations to its workpeople, which the Institute was evidence. On the other hand, it expected the men to fill their obligations towards the company; he hoped the men felt the club belonged to them; that it was there for their happiness and convenience. He hoped there would never be any cause for the company to regret having built such a beautiful place for the use of the workmen of Mansfield Colliery.* [11]

At the time of the official opening, the Forest Town Institute already had a number of athletic and other organisations.

A cricket club had been formed and the team being put together included;

J. Bingley (Colliery Manager),
Poole (Belfast),
White (late of Notts.),
Barnes, and others.

Around 45 fixtures had already been arranged for the coming season, not just with the many clubs around the district, but also those much further afield including Skegness.

Bowling was another activity and it was predicted that a bowling club would soon be arranging matches with other local greens.

A horticultural society was to be developed. A show and sports were being arranged, and for this event, the band of the Queen's Own Yorkshire Dragoons had been engaged. Over £100 prize money had been allocated for the show and the sports.

Cycle races were to be held throughout the season and frequent concerts were to be arranged. Events like these continued for many years in Forest Town and the events on the cycle track are still talked about today.

When the Mansfield Colliery Institute opened in 1908, membership was four shillings (20p) a year. Membership was for men only. John P. Houfton general manager of the Bolsover Colliery Company was the Institute's president, J. Bingley vice-president, and T. W. Shore the secretary.

By October 1910 membership was still just four shillings (20p), and the Institute now had over four hundred members. However by this date, ladies were allowed to use the library which was well stocked with around 400 books. They could also use the reading room. To be eligible for this, the ladies had to be members of the Tennis Club, for which the membership fee was five shillings (25p) a year.[12]

Facilities around the grounds had expanded, and members could now play croquet as well as tennis. The cinder cycle track was attracting a number of eminent local cyclists including Harvey who was the twice Midland Champion. At sports held

The tennis courts which also show the well laid out gardens.

A cycling event on the Miners' Institute track.

in August 1910, on the cycle track Harvey won the half mile scratch race. The tug-of-war team was reputed to be the 'Best in the Midlands'. Captained by P. Davis, they had recently won the Bainbridge Silver Challenge Cup in a contest at Hucknall.[13]

By 1911, the Institute had numerous officials and committee members;

President - *Mr J. P. Houfton.*

Vice Presidents
Messrs T. N. Tatlow, J. Bingley, A. Davis, P. W. Philips, J. Severn, and J. Tebbett.

Treasurer - *Mr T. Wakefield.*

Secretary - *Mr T. W.Share.* **Assistant Secretary** - *Mr J. Murden.*

Caretaker - *Mr R. Blount.*

Committee
Messrs *J. Sales, T. Boden, W. Hargreaves, J. Annable, J. Withers, W. Birkett, R. Dunn, G. Gittings, J. Barnes, J. Hopewell, H. North, T. Bosworth.*

The Cricket Club who were becoming well established were the holders of the Houfton inter-Colliery Challenge Cup. The first eleven, who were in the Bassetlaw League were captained by J. Bingley. The second eleven were in the Portland League, and their captain is unknown.

Presidents and officials of the Cricket Club included:

O. J. Bainbridge
J. A. Bell
J. Bingley
A. Brain
W. Cook
A. Davis
T. Fairfield
A. Gabbitas
C. Hardwick
C. Houfton
Dr Houfton
J. P. Houfton
W. O. Houfton
R. L. Jones
A. Lees
M. Meany
J. Murden
P. W. Philips
G. Place
W. Richmond
J. Sales
T. W. Share
A. Wakefield
T. Wakefield

The grounds around the Forest Town Miners' Institute were very spacious, and it is not surprising that there were occasions when sport and the sound of brass bands went together. One such event took place in June 1911 when Mansfield Colliery were playing cricket against a team from Whitwell. A bowls match and a brass band contest was also taking place. It was the occasion of the third annual contest with the Mansfield Colliery Band, and Mr J. Bryer of Leicester was the adjudicator. However the wonderful sound of cornets, trombones, euphonium and other instruments came to a temporary halt when a thunderstorm broke out and 'rain stopped play'.

Eventually the decision was made to abandon both the cricket and bowls but the musicians in their distinguishable uniforms resumed playing, and the competition continued. The Lincoln Malleable's won the Challenge Cup given by Mansfield Colliery for the third year in succession, and other winners on the day were Grimethorpe, Colwyn, and Swanwick.[14]

Colliery bands were an important part of village life, and there was possibly a lot of truth in the saying that 'if you could play an instrument you could always get a job at the colliery.' Most families in the village had at least one or two members who played in the band. The men were proud of their instruments, and they enjoyed the frequent music practises and the competitions.

A good bandmaster was important and the earliest known bandmaster in Forest Town was Jack Cupit, he had previously been a bandmaster with the Hucknall Excelsior Temperance Prize Band.[15] The exact date Jack Cupit came to Forest Town is unknown, but as a number of Cupit families were in the village in 1906 it is possible he was one of them. He is listed in the Linneys Directories for 1911, and 1912 under Forest Town as the 'Bandmaster of the Silver Prize Band', also at that time K. Annable is named as the Secretary.[16]

Very little information on the band(s) is available, and it is believed there was both a Mansfield Colliery Silver Prize Band and a Mansfield Colliery Band. Harry (Henry) Roulston was another bandmaster of these that is still remembered locally. Harry had previously played for many years in a band at Woodville, near Burton-on-Trent. He played BBb (B flat double bass). He is believed to have moved to Forest Town around 1914 and lived in the Avenues.[17]

The Colliery Band with Bandmaster Jack Cupit with the cup

Harry Roulston, behind the shield with the Mansfield Colliery Band circa 1931

There were many enjoyable band concerts in the grounds of the new Institute and the opportunity of 'light' refreshment when the players had performed their rousing tunes.

Over the years the premises were looked after by various stewards such as G. Hill 1913, and Mr & Mrs H. A. Daxon 1916 - 1930. Mrs Daxon and a team of ladies did the catering at many events in the village.

Mr & Mrs Daxon

Inside the Institute building, the large concert hall was an ideal venue for 'annual dinners.' In December 1914, the annual dinner of the Cricket and Bowling Clubs took place. This was only a few months after King George V and Queen Mary had visited Forest Town, and after the outbreak of war had taken place. While those events were not forgotten, an emphasis was placed on the sporting achievements of the past season. John P. Houfton, in his speech as chairman said 'the colliery matches brought out the best sporting instincts of the players, and it was something of a credit to the company that they were so proficient in sports.' There followed many references to both the players and the events:

> *There was an exciting end to the matches played for the Houfton Cup which was won by Mansfield Colliery. C. N. Newcombe (now a Lieutenant in the KOYLI) had the best batting average of 58. T. Poole won the bowling with 10.8.*
>
> *Mansfield Colliery were also the winners of the Portland Cup (the Portland League Trophy) donated by the Duke of Portland. Added to this they won medals, and C. Turner headed the batting with 47.14. followed by J. White with 36.25. The bowling being won by G. Wass 7.74, and A. Warren 8.5.* [18]

Special reference was made when referring to the Notts. League of players to those who were now serving with the colours. These included:

C. N. Newcombe	(KOYLI.)
C. A. Turner	8th Reserve Bat. Sherwood Foresters.
C. Chester	8th Reserve Bat. Sherwood Foresters.

The presentation list reveals many names, some who are still recalled in Forest Town today

CRICKET CLUB

O. Alexandra	*G. Annable*	*J. Barnes*
A. Boot	*A. Buxton*	*G. Chester*
J. Chester	*W. Cooper*	*J. Cutts*
W. Davis	*T. Elvidge*	*T. Milnes*
J. Murden	*W. Peters*	*T. Poole*
J. Purdy	*J. Rice*	*A. Saxton*
W. Smith	*W. Tomlinson*	*A. Warren*
G. Wass	*J. White*	*W. W. Whysall*

BOWLING

J. Barlow	*T. Fox*	*G. Gittings*
W. Hargreaves	*W. Hickman*	*D. Johnson*
R. Silcock	*H. Mellows*	*W.(A. S.) Marklew*
E. Naylor	*E.W. Naylor*	*F. Pearson*
T. Share	*G. Smith*	*T. Wakefield*
E. Walker		

WHIST COMPETITION PRIZE-WINNERS

T. Bosworth	(6 Spoons)	*W. H. Carter*	(Vase)
T. Fairfield	(6 Spoons)	*D. Johnson*	(Pint Tankard)
J. Needham	(Half-pint Tankard)	*A. Parker*	(6 spoons)
J. Sefton	(Cruet)	*J. White*	(6 Spoons)

The evening ended with musical entertainment from

Messrs N. Holland, J. Handley, J. Woolrich, and W. Hickman.

Throughout the years of the First World War, the Institute would have had many sombre moments when tragic news of local lads serving in the war was heard. If tough miners shed tears, then no doubt a few would have been spilt in their pints of beer! However it was not all gloom, for the Institute had its own part to play in the war. Over the war years, the hospitality of both the building and grounds was offered to the soldiers from Clipstone Camp, a large military training camp erected near Forest Town. The soldiers were often seen playing in cricket matches, and participating in other sporting events. They were also a reminder of what was happening in the wider world.

Despite the war, local sports events were still an attraction and moral booster for the community. On a fine day, early in July 1918, over 2,000 people attended the Mansfield Colliery Boys' Brigade sports on the cricket ground. There were many events:

Handicap Flat Race, Brass Band Race, Tug-of-War,
Three Leg Race, High Jump, Sack Race,
Tilting the Bucket, and one Mile Flat Race.

A Pony Drivers race, with pit pony and tub on specially laid rail attracted 71 entries and six competed in the final. The winners were

1st *W. Cutts* - 1min 6 secs
2nd *H. Wharmby* - 1min 9 secs
3rd *R. Purdy* - 1min 12½ secs.

Possibly the above event.

The music of the Mansfield Colliery Prize Band added to the atmosphere of the day. With Harry Roulston conducting they played marches, overtures, waltzes and other selections much to everyone's enjoyment.

Suddenly, around 4:30pm on that afternoon, a noise of a very different kind was heard. For the hundreds of people present, it was a noise not heard before; as they sat on the banks of the field they became aware of a flying machine coming towards Forest Town. As the aircraft approached the sports ground, the engines slowed down and the airman first circled the ground, then did a spiral over the village gardens, he returned to give a final salute and then flew on his way. The excited crowd learnt that the airman was Major Brown of the Royal Air Force, who had once been a member of the Forest Town Boys Brigade.[19]

Within a few weeks of that exciting day, the Mansfield Colliery Cricket Club held its first sports event since 1914. Once again, the instruments of the Mansfield Colliery Prize Band were to be heard rousing everyone with their music. Among the competitors were soldiers from the Clipstone Camp, and additional to the various flat races were relay and obstacle races, tug-of-war and cycle events, with cyclists racing distances of half a mile, three quarters of a mile and one mile.[20]

While occasions such as these were good for the morale of the community, the Institute also played its part in more sombre occasions. The grounds were large enough for the village people to gather together, and on the 6th July 1919 there was a scene of a more solemn and celebratory event, the Forest Town Peace Thanksgiving.

The village, was paraded by a procession, consisting of all the children led by the colliery band, followed by the Boys' Brigade and Cadets, with Bugle Band, special constables, and the demobilised sailors and soldiers who turned out in full force. [21]

The procession ended in the grounds of the Institute, to join many people from both the village and surrounding communities for a united service led by Rev H. Bull (St Alban's Church), Mr A. Shaw (Primitive Methodist), and Mr G. Lee (Wesleyan Methodist). United choirs took part, and the Colliery Band played music before and after the service.

It may have been on this occasion when many young people in the village were given a Peace Memento card.

These displayed the flags of the allied forces in bright colours, and each had the name of the person they were given to written on it.

Eleven years prior to the Peace Parade, when the Bolsover Colliery Company had built the new Institute in Forest Town, no one could have foreseen the future. At the official opening in 1908, Oswald Bainbridge said that he hoped the men would take full advantage of the new premises and facilities, those words had a far greater meaning than anyone at that time realised. The Institute provided not just facilities for men; it was an important asset to the whole community and this continued until it was demolished in the early 1960s. It was replaced with the present Miners Welfare Building in 1970.[22]

The Old and the New Institute Buildings

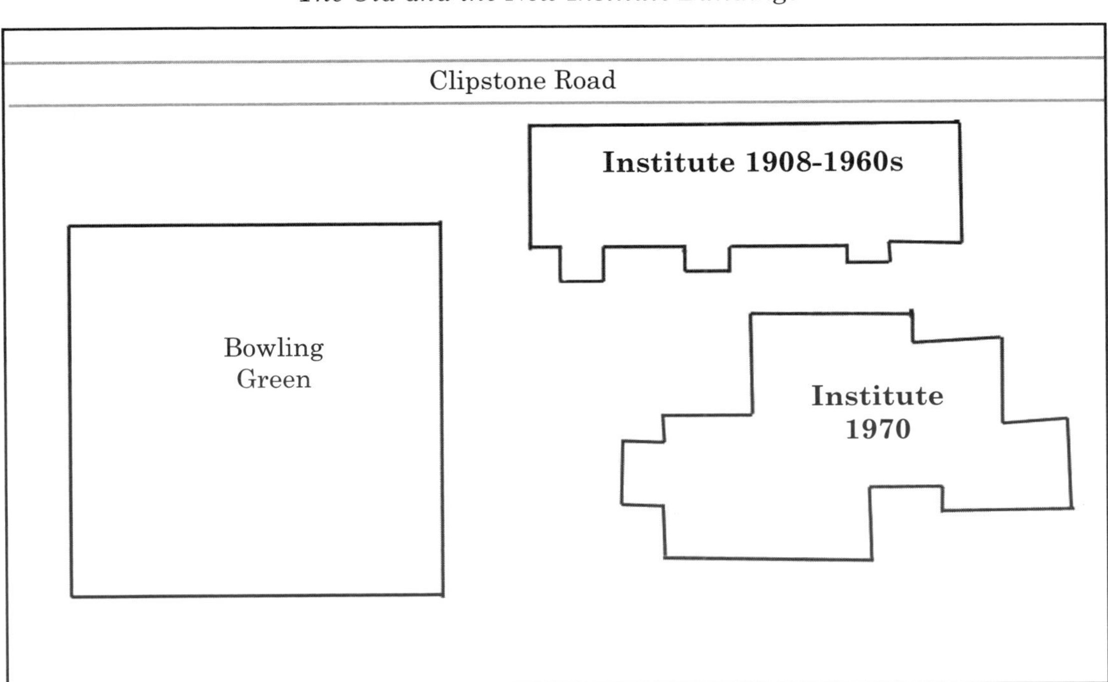

NOTES

1. Colliery Guardian December 1969, article 'A Page of Mining History' by W. H. N. Carter CBE.
2. Derbyshire Times 3 June 1905.
3. In many mining communities the Miners' Welfare Institute is referred to as the 'Club'.
4. Oral history Arthur Parker and other people in Forest Town.
5. NA DCMW 3/9/10/1.
6. Mansfield Reporter 10 April 1908.
7. Mansfield & North Notts Advertiser 16 August 1907.
8. Mansfield & North Notts Advertiser 13 September 1907.
9. Mansfield Reporter 10 April 1908.
10. As above.
11. As above.
12. The Courier 15 October 1910.
13. As above.
14. Notts Free Press 23 June 1911.
15. Information from Mr & Mrs Baker.
16. Linneys Almanac 1911 & 1912.
17. Notes from Neil Roe/A. Hewitt.
18. The _____ & Sutton Times 4 December 1914.
19. Mansfield Chronicle Advertiser 5 July 1918.
20. Mansfield & Sutton Reporter 30 August 1918.
21. Mansfield & North Notts Advertiser 11 July 1919.
22. Club facilities were held in the Drill Hall after the Institute was demolished and the new one built.

15 - THE DRILL HALL

As the village of Forest Town grew, the recreational needs of the local community were considered by the Bolsover Colliery Company. At the time the Welfare Institute was built to provide social facilities for the workmen, amenities for younger people were also being planned. When in April 1908 a Mansfield newspaper reported on the opening of the New Welfare Institute in Forest Town, it additionally told the readers

The efforts of the company on behalf of their workmen do not end here, for a contract has just been let for the building of a Boys' Brigade Hall, and Club at the other end of the village. The cost is estimated at £3,000 and the Duke of Portland who is taking a personal interest in the project, has promised to give £500 towards the expense.[1]

The hall the article referred to became known as the Drill Hall. It was erected on open land with the terraced houses of First and Second Avenue standing adjacent to the grounds, while to the rear, and just over the main Clipstone Road, stood the Methodist Church and the Travellers Rest Farm.

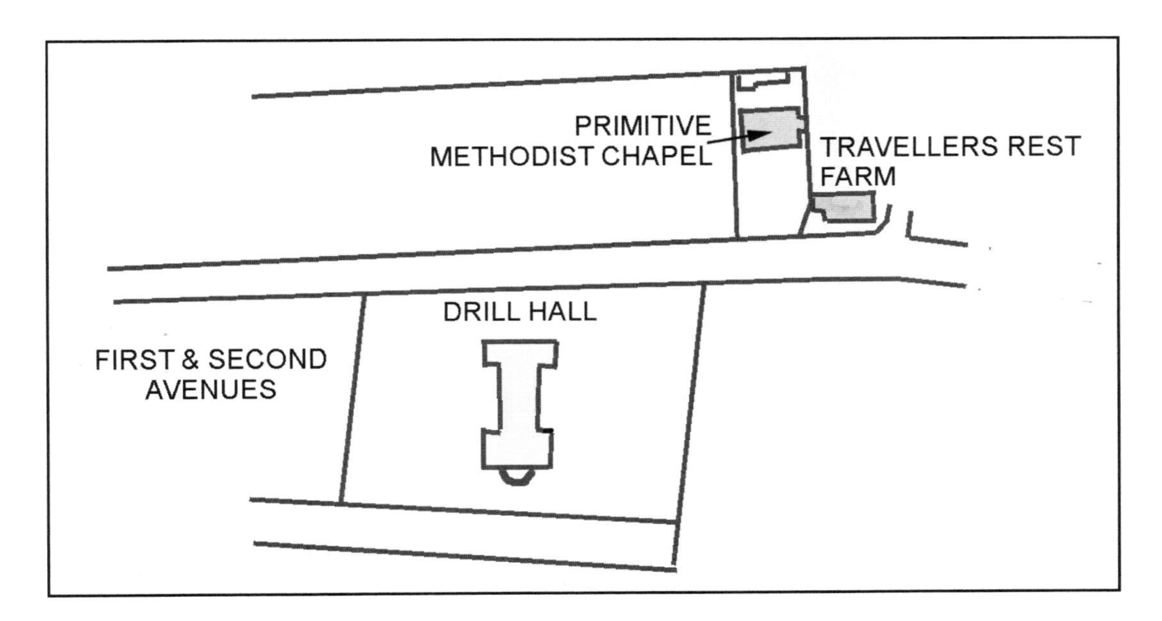

The impressive new building was built of brick and not surprisingly, hence its name, featured a large drill hall 60' x 36' [18.288m x 10.973m]. The hall despite housing gymnastic apparatus, was also intended to be used for various kinds of public entertainment. It had an open timber roof and panelled walls and these panels adorned the side of a recessed stage which were enriched with plaster moulding. Rooms at each side of the stage were referred to as ladies and gentlemen's retiring rooms, (dressing rooms). Additionally on the ground floor there were four other rooms adjacent to the main entrance, to be used for recreation such as reading, the boys cricket club and billiards.

An elegant staircase, Georgian in character, rose to the upper floor commencing with a double flight of stairs that met at a half landing where they continued to the first floor. The first floor landing opened out to a balcony, which made an interesting feature over the front entrance of the building. Wide stone mullion bay windows, and spacious single fireplaces gave additional character to some of the rooms of the impressive building.[2]

The official opening of the Drill Hall took place at 3 o'clock in the afternoon on Saturday the 15th May 1909. The weather was reported to be favourable with the exception of a cold wind. Well before the appointed time large crowds were gathering to watch the proceedings, among them were miners with their wives and families, smartly dressed as befitted the occasion, with visitors from Bolsover, Creswell and Mansfield.

Appropriate to the opening of a Drill Hall, contingents of the Colliery Boys' Brigade were assembled to proudly form a guard of honour along the road to the new building. One hundred and thirty of these were from Mansfield supported by one hundred and forty from Creswell. Sir William Robson, M.P. the Attorney General on National Defence, accompanied by Mr Emerson Muschamp Bainbridge, chairman of the Bolsover Colliery Company, was saluted by the Boys' Brigade as he walked to perform the opening ceremony of the new hall.[3] The smartness and colour of the uniforms of the Boys' Brigade, and the two colliery bands, who were also present, would have been a pleasing sight.

Waiting under the balcony entrance was Mr Percy Bond Houfton, the architect of the Drill Hall building, and he presented Sir William with a silver guilt key to formally open the door. Once the opening ceremony had taken place, the official party, guests, miners, and members of the brigade, proceeded into the hall. Inside on the flower-bedecked stage, members of the Mansfield Colliery Band played appropriate music as everyone took their places.

The proceedings began with singing of 'Onward Christian Soldiers,' and was then followed by a prayer, read by Rev. E. T. Harcombe. It is not hard to visualise the hearty singing of this rousing hymn, followed by the solemn quiet of meaningful prayer. All eyes and ears were then focused on Mr Emerson Bainbridge, Sir William Robson, and the other dignitaries who gave speeches; these also included the Duke of Portland's agent, Mr Warner Turner; the general manager of the Bolsover Colliery Company, Mr John P. Houfton; Mr J. Bingley, Mr A. Davis, manager and undermanager of the Mansfield Colliery and Mr Oswald Bainbridge.[4] Sir William Robson was then presented with a photograph album that contained pictures of Forest Town, the colliery, and other buildings.

During the course of the afternoon's events, there was also musical entertainment given by four well known singers, A. W. Kingston, W. H. Kingston, H. Henderson and W. Holland. Alfred W. Kingston was already becoming well known for his powerful singing voice. On that afternoon, he sang two solos, 'Nirvanna' and 'I hear you calling' which received special compliments from the chairman, Emerson Bainbridge.[5]

The afternoon ended with the young lads of the Boys' Brigade lining up for a final inspection by Sir William Robson. The visitors, bandsmen, and the brigades then had tea in two large marquees outside the hall.[6]

Two photographs taken at the opening of the Drill Hall.

On the reverse of the top one (a postcard) the sender wrote
'I am sending a card with the procession on the way to the Drill Hall, that was opened a few weeks ago, you can just see the club house in the back ground of 2nd Ave... The lady in the centre of the picture is Mrs Bainbridge from Sherwood Hall, the gentleman opened the Drill Hall that stands on her right side and her husband and her father and their guest on her left.'

The Drill Hall was the headquarters for the Mansfield Colliery Boys' Brigade. The Bolsover Colliery Company believed it had an obligation to encourage young lads to use their leisure time wisely. It was assumed that by drilling them at an early age, they would begin to form units who would move on into the cadet corps and ambulance corps. Some would even go into the Territorial Army, and for many of the young lads, the principles they learnt as a member of the Boys' Brigade helped them to be better citizens in their adult lives.[7]

The Boys Brigade Badge is on the fireplace hood in the former Drill Hall, now Kingsway Hall

By October 1910 the Boys' Brigade had a thriving membership. Officers of the brigade were;

Captain *Mr J. Bingley*; Adjutant *Mr Aaron Bircumshaw.*
First Lieuts. *Messrs W. Kingston and J. E. Senior.*
Second Lieuts. *Messrs P. Houghton and J. Hinton.*

The numerical strength was reported as being;

7 Commissioned Officers, 12 Non-commissioned Officers, 180 Rank and File.
18 Bugle Band, making a grand total of 217.
There was an additional membership of 70 in the Cadet Corps.[8]

Over the next few years, there were changes to the names of officers and ranks and these now came under a combined heading of Mansfield Colliery Boys' Brigade and Cadet Corps. They all met at the Drill Hall.

1912 Major *J. Bingley,* Adjutant, *W. Kingston.*
Capts. *J. A. Severn and J. E. Senior.*
First Lieuts. *J. A. Staton and J. Hinton.*
Second Lieuts. *W. Parr and W. H. Mein.*
Instructors Sergt. - Major *Lacey and R. Beresford.*

1914 Major *W. Carter;*
Capts. *W. H. Kingston, and J Hinton.*
First Lieuts. *J. A. Staton and W. Parr.*
Second Lieuts. *F. Smart and C. Turner.*
Instructor, Sergt.-Major *C. A. Lacey.*
Bugle Band Instructor, *F. Munnings.*
Hon. Surgeon, *E. H. Houfton MD.*
Hon Chaplain, *Rev H. Bull*[9]

Life in the Boys' Brigade and Cadets was not just a routine of drill and bugle practise, there were gymnasium activities and games such as billiards. Additionally there was the opportunity to play in cricket and football clubs. The lads, their activities and equipment would have been well known to the caretaker of the Drill Hall who for many years was G. Brown. A highlight of the year's activities was the annual camp to places such as Bridlington, Skegness and Yarmouth. These events are still talked about in the village today and were sometimes noted in the local papers;

> Mansfield & North Notts Reporter 5th August 1910 - *Mansfield Colliery Boys' Brigade and cadets, 190 strong returned home Thursday last after a week under canvas at Yarmouth.*

The newspaper told of how on the Sunday the Church Parade had been to St Nicholas' Church and a selection of marches had been played en route under the leadership of Bandmaster J. Cupit.

At an unknown date, possibly in the 1920's, a division of the Girls' Brigade was formed. This enthusiastic group also enjoyed the facilities of the Drill Hall for many years and went on annual camp. Additionally they produced concerts (such as the one below), for the entertainment of others, and the Drill Hall with its stage and dressing rooms was the ideal venue.

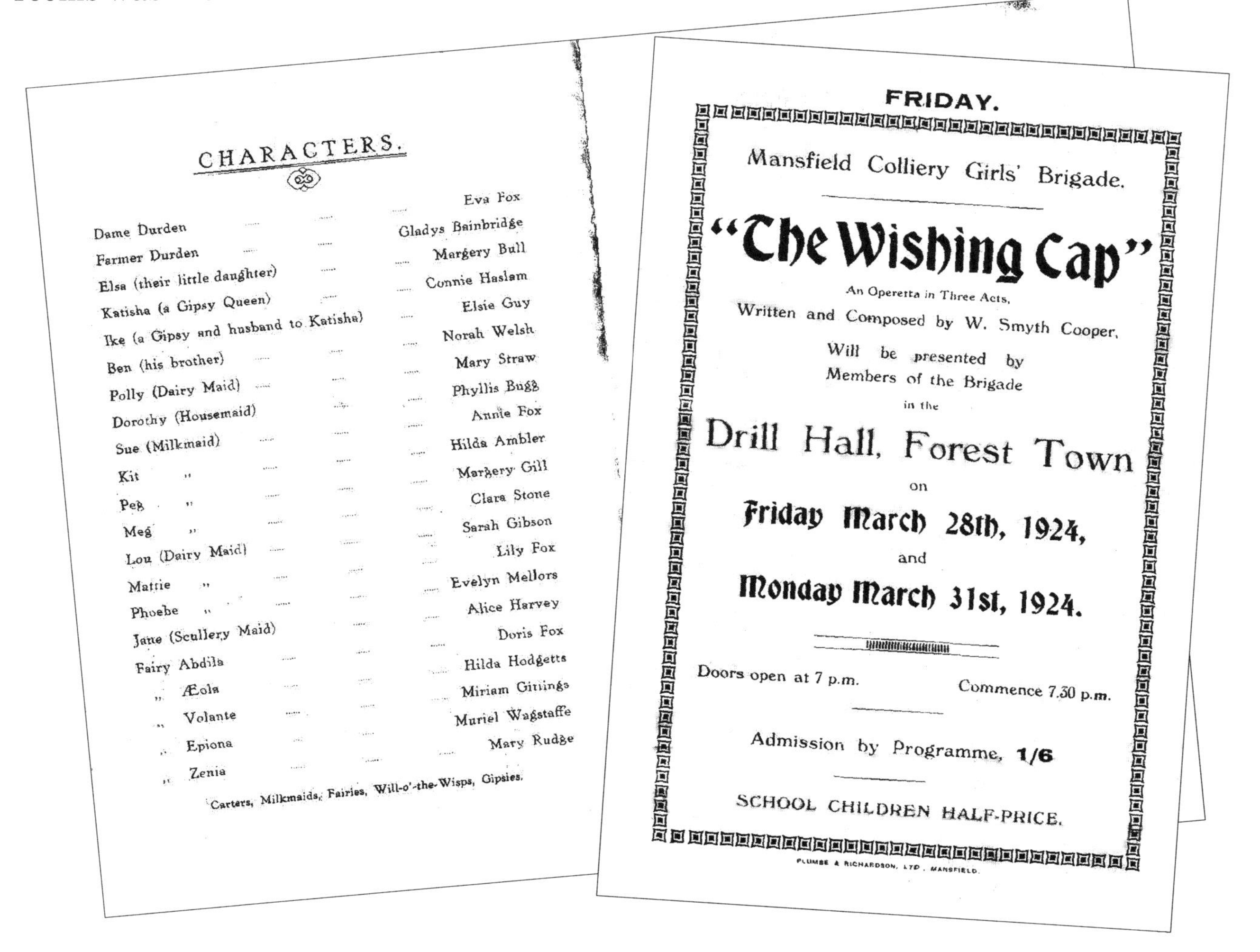

CHARACTERS.

Character	Performer
Dame Durden	Eva Fox
Farmer Durden	Gladys Bainbridge
Elsa (their little daughter)	Margery Bull
Katisha (a Gipsy Queen)	Connie Haslam
Ike (a Gipsy and husband to Katisha)	Elsie Guy
Ben (his brother)	Norah Welsh
Polly (Dairy Maid)	Mary Straw
Dorothy (Housemaid)	Phyllis Bugg
Sue (Milkmaid)	Annie Fox
Kit ,,	Hilda Ambler
Peg ,,	Margery Gill
Meg ,,	Clara Stone
Lou (Dairy Maid)	Sarah Gibson
Mattie ,,	Lily Fox
Phoebe ,,	Evelyn Mellors
Jane (Scullery Maid)	Alice Harvey
Fairy Abdila	Doris Fox
,, Æola	Hilda Hodgetts
,, Volante	Miriam Gittings
,, Epiona	Muriel Wagstaffe
,, Zenia	Mary Rudge

Carters, Milkmaids, Fairies, Will-o'-the-Wisps, Gipsies.

FRIDAY.

Mansfield Colliery Girls' Brigade.

"The Wishing Cap"

An Operetta in Three Acts,

Written and Composed by W. Smyth Cooper,

Will be presented by Members of the Brigade in the

Drill Hall, Forest Town

on

Friday March 28th, 1924,

and

Monday March 31st, 1924.

Doors open at 7 p.m. Commence 7.30 p.m.

Admission by Programme, 1/6

SCHOOL CHILDREN HALF-PRICE.

PLUMBE & RICHARDSON, LTD., MANSFIELD.

The front of the Drill Hall from the right (above) and from the left (below)

While for many years the Drill Hall was well patronised by different groups attached to the Mansfield Colliery, it was also used by the village community for a wide variety of other purposes.

From June 1909, the Wesleyan Methodists held their services in the Drill Hall; a special service was held to inaugurate the use of the hall for this purpose. They eventually moved into their own purpose built chapel on land adjacent to the Drill Hall.[10]

In November 1910, after a stone laying ceremony on the site of the new St Alban's Church, a tea for approximately 300 people was served in the Drill Hall. The day's events concluded when the St Alban's Glee Club entertained at a dance and social in the evening.[11]

In September 1914, great scenes prevailed in the village where the focus of the excitement was the Drill Hall. At short notice, a meeting had been called, and the colliery band had paraded round the streets signalling the importance of the occasion and encouraging everyone to assemble at the Drill Hall. It was on this occasion when many young men were encouraged to enlist and fight for King and Country.[12]

Throughout the years since the opening in 1909, dances, whist drives, concerts, and bazaars are just some of the events that have taken place inside the building. Outside the grounds are remembered as having nice gardens and being well kept. It is a place that was well loved by people in the community.

Patrons & Committee Joint Winners Earl Haigh Cup 1922
Standing; G. Cutts, J. Gamble, J. Caddy, E. Day, E. Mott, J. O'Meara, A. S. Peters (Hon Sec.), A. Ward, G. Wright, T. Watson, W. Barthorpe
Seated; L. B. Taylor (Branch Chairman), J. Lee DCM & Bar (Branch President) W. H. Carter, F. Davis, Rev Bull.

Well remembered too is a backcloth on the stage, which suggests the patronage of the Duke of Portland had not gone unnoticed, for despite being the local landowner, the Duke encouraged and supported things he believed in, and as a former military man the Drill Hall would have fallen into this category. It is possible that the elaborate backdrop was painted with the Duke in mind. It showed the 'Russian Hut' an interesting wooden building which belonged to the Duke on his local estate.

There are many theories as to who painted the backdrop, and also what happened to it, the truth it seems remains in the past, with the history of the Forest Town Drill Hall.[13]

NOTES

1 Mansfield Reporter 10 April 1908.
2 Mansfield Advertiser 14 May 1909.
3 Mansfield & North Notts Advertiser 21 May 1909.
4 As above.
5 As above.
6 As above.
7 Extract from un-named paper.
8 The Courier 15 October 1910.
9 Linneys Almanac.
10 Mansfield & North Notts Advertiser 11 June 1909.
11 Mansfield & North Notts Advertiser 11 Nov 1910.
12 Mansfield Reporter 11 September 1914.
13 The Drill Hall eventually became known as Kingsway Hall. It is still in use today (2005).

16 - THE SINGING MINER

The early years of Forest Town were an age when people had to entertain themselves, or as some did, entertained others. Many village people enjoyed listening to a variety of musicians, and vocalists at events in and around the area. Anyone with a musical ability would receive encouragement to participate in local activities or, in some cases to improve their talent. For most of these local artists, singing or playing musical instruments was additional to their normal everyday working life, and many of them worked at the colliery. One such person was Alfred Webster Kingston, he was often to be heard at local events, and his strong tenor voice delighted many an audience. This Mansfield Colliery miner soon became well known to the people of Forest Town, and the surrounding area.

Like many of the other miners he was not a local man. Alfred was born at Wednesbury, Staffordshire in 1875, the third son of John and Jane Kingston. By April 1881 the family had moved to live in Hucknall, Nottinghamshire, where as the census shows his father was a coal miner.

Name		*Age*	*Occupation*	*Where Born*
John Kingston	Head	32	Coal Miner	STF Tipton
Jane Kingston	Wife	30	-------	STF Tipton
John T Kingston	Son	9	Scholar	STF Tipton
William Kingston	Son	7	Scholar	STF Tipton
Alfred Kingston	Son	6	Scholar	STF Wednesbury

1881 Census Piece No. 3335 Folio 86 - Beardall Street, Hucknall, Nottinghamshire.

The Kingston boys are reputed to have attended school in Hucknall, and St John's Parish Church, where Alfred was said to have been a chorister. John and Jane Kingston had two more children, who were born in Hucknall, Frederick and Elizabeth. The family continued to live in Beardall Street. Like many young boys in those days William and Alfred left school at an early age, Alfred was believed to have been just ten. Like their father both boys worked at the coal mine in Hucknall.[1]

These two brothers had a talent for singing and became part of the Byron Quartet, along with William Holland,[2] and H. G. M. Henderson.[3] At the age of fourteen Alfred had joined the Hucknall Torkard Brass Band playing the tenor horn. Through his training with the band he gained a knowledge of operas and oratorios. He bought a piano and taught himself music more seriously.

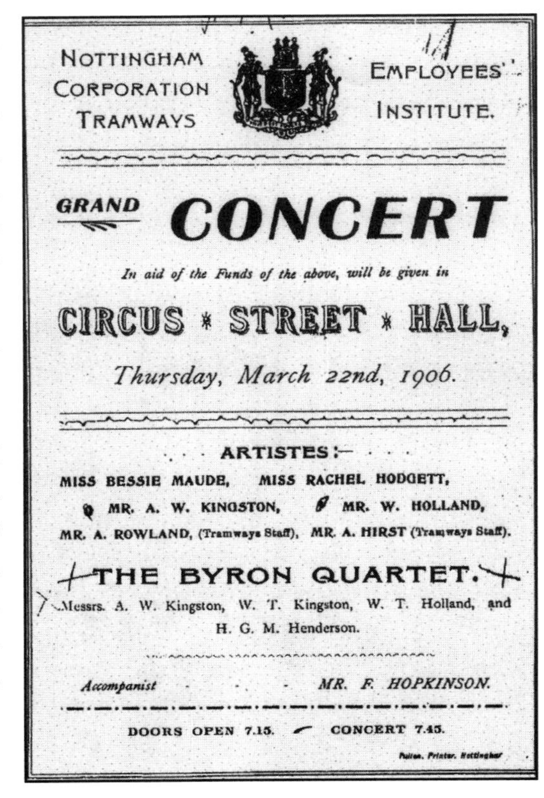

He began singing publicly around the age of eighteen, his first concert was in Nottingham and he was an instant success and more concerts followed.[4] However during this period Alfred Kingston's main occupation was that of a coal miner.

Morgan Kingston taken from the cover of a concert in Nottinghamshire 1912.

It was around 1906 when both Alfred and William, along with other miners, decided to leave the pits in Hucknall to work at Mansfield (Crown Farm) Colliery. The new coalfields at Mansfield had obviously more to offer. Alfred was by this time married with a family of his own, and on moving to Mansfield first lived on St Margaret Street. They later moved to a house on Carter Lane, just a short distance from Forest Town and Alfred's work at the colliery.

Alfred's talent for singing soon became well known, and he began appearing at many events around the area.

In December 1907, he sang at the Victoria Hall, Mansfield, the occasion was St Peter's Church bazaar, an event held over three days and complimented by evening entertainment. The bazaar was to raise funds for the building of the new church of St Lawrence, this was not far from Carter Lane where Alfred Kingston lived.

Since the sinking of Mansfield Colliery the whole area had seen a growth in population and building development. In June 1908, another fund-raising social and musical entertainment was held, when the contract for the new St Lawrence's Church was awarded to T. & R. Moore. Once again Alfred Kingston was reported 'to be in splendid voice and his rendering of "Nirvana" and "My Queen" was quite equal to anything previously heard from this talented singer.' His songs, it seems were greatly appreciated, and 'he brought down the house.'[5]

No doubt some of the people living in Forest Town and representatives from the colliery would have attended these events, they also had opportunities to listen to this local miner with the powerful singing voice at events in their own village.

The opening of the Drill Hall in May 1909 was said to be a very splendid and festive occasion, with the Boys' Brigade forming a guard of honour and Sir William Robson, the Attorney General on National Defence, performing the opening ceremony. The streets were lined with miners and their families; many colliery officials and civic dignitaries were present, and Mansfield Colliery Band provided music. It was also an occasion in which noted local singers participated, among these was the powerful singing voice of Alfred Kingston. This was acknowledged by the chairman Mr Emerson Bainbridge, (the owner of the Bolsover Colliery Company):

During the proceedings, Messrs A. W. Kingston, W. H. Kingston, H. Henderson and W. Holland sang with excellent effect 'Comrades in Arms' and Mr A. W. Kingston gave in splendid style "Nirvanna" and "I Hear You Calling." The chairman complimenting the singer and congratulating Forest Town upon having such a fine vocalist as Mr A. W. Kingston.[6]

In July 1911 the Bishop of Southwell consecrated the new Church of St Alban's, and throughout the day there were various services and ceremonies. At the evening service, Archdeacon Richardson was said to have preached a powerful sermon to a crowded congregation. However powerful his voice was, one wonders if it matched the strong tenor voice of Alfred Kingston, for he was reputed to have sung in 'a masterful manner' at the service, and it was enjoyed by all present.[7]

By that time Alfred Kingston had plenty to sing about, for additional to working at Mansfield Colliery he was now studying music in London. This occurred when a few years previously Albert Davis the undermanager at Mansfield Colliery, had introduced him to Rev. Stainer, a curate at Warsop Vale Parish Church. A request to sing at the Warsop church bazaar eventually led to an introduction to people in the right circles in London who were keen to encourage him to develop his singing voice.[8]

This was a great step forward for the miner who loved to sing. During the early days of his training in London, Alfred Kingston continued to work at Mansfield Colliery. It was said he would work a double shift to pay for his fare to London and his singing lessons.[9] This could not have been easy in those days, especially for a married man with children.

However, his hard work, plus the encouragement of his friends and colleagues was amply rewarded when in December 1909 he made his singing debut at the Queens Hall, London.[10] Albert Davis, William Holland, and other friends travelled to London for this great occasion.

This was no doubt the turning point in the life of this colliery worker, for within three years he was singing in America.

This theatre, when filled to its capacity can be emptied in five minutes. Choose the nearest exit now and in case of need walk quietly (do not run) to that exit in order to avoid panic

METROPOLITAN OPERA HOUSE

GRAND OPERA SEASON 1917~1918
GIULIO GATTI-CASAZZA, General Manager.

SATURDAY EVENING, DECEMBER 1ST, AT 8 O'CLOCK

IL TROVATORE

OPERA IN FOUR ACTS AND EIGHT SCENES
BOOK BY SALVATORE CAMMARANO
(IN ITALIAN)
MUSIC BY GIUSEPPE VERDI

LEONORA . . . . CLAUDIA MUZIO
AZUCENA . . . . MARGARETE MATZENAUER
INEZ . . . . MARIE MATTFELD
MANRICO . . . . MORGAN KINGSTON
HIS FIRST APPEARANCE AT THE METROPOLITAN OPERA HOUSE
COUNT DI LUNA . . . . GIUSEPPE DE LUCA
FERRANDO . . . . LEON ROTHIER
RUIZ . . . . PIETRO AUDISIO
A GIPSY . . . . VINCENZO RESCHIGLIAN
CONDUCTOR . . . . GENNARO PAPI

STAGE DIRECTOR . . . . RICHARD ORDYNSKI
CHORUS MASTER . . . . GIULIO SETTI
TECHNICAL DIRECTOR . . . . EDWARD SIEDLE
STAGE MANAGER . . . . ARMANDO F. AGNINI

PROGRAMME CONTINUED ON NEXT PAGE

CORRECT LIBRETTOS FOR SALE IN THE LOBBY

HARDMAN PIANOS USED EXCLUSIVELY

On September 13th 1913 he made his American debut as *Ramades* in *Aida* with the Century Opera Company, New York. Between 1917 and 1924 he sang with the Metropolitan Opera Company, New York.

MR. MORGAN KINGSTON

FROM COALMINE TO GRAND OPERA

The Times 8 August 1936

It is evident that the name Alfred Kingston did not create the right image of an opera singer, and he became known professionally as Morgan Kingston. It has been suggested that the name Morgan was chosen because it implied this former miner with the impressive singing voice had a Welsh background![11] His early life in the colliery does appear to have helped him develop both the character and stature for his operatic career, as an American music journalist once wrote of him;

> *'he has the strength of a bullock, and the lithe gracefulness and quickness of a panther. He is broad shouldered, deep of chest, and, according to accounts from mining districts on the other side, he has a regular John Jefferies of a punch in either hand. He has a set of biceps that added realism to the part of Samson which he recently played in Samson and Delilah. If he hadn't been a singer, he could have made a fortune as a professional strong man.'*[12]

Morgan Kingston also told journalists that while he was a fine boxer he had plenty of exercise working in the pit, and so any spare time he had was taken up with music. He did not believe that hard work injured anyone's voice and he had 'always taken his share of the work with the other men on the coal face, and ever since he was a little pony driver he had been a user of tobacco.'[13]

After enjoying seven or eight seasons with the Metropolitan Opera Company, Morgan Kingston returned to England, and sang at Covent Garden, London in June 1924, and the Albert Hall in 1925. It is said that he was always appreciative of his friends and colleagues in Nottinghamshire, and he did not forget the people of Mansfield. In February 1926 he was given a civic welcome when he returned to sing in the Fourth Stephenson Subscription Concert at Mansfield. He delighted the audience with his renderings of:

Lohengrin's Farewell (Wagner), *The Dying Harper* (Schindler), *Prelude* from the *Cycle of Life* (Landon Ronald), *Vesti la Gubba* from Leconvalle's *Pagliacci* and finally *Nirvana* (Stephen Adams).

The career of this former Mansfield Colliery miner extended to making records, and during 1913 -1917 he was recording with the Columbia Record Company. These records are now highly sought after, especially in America.

Singing Miner Dies.

Notts. Man Who Became Famous.

Mr. Morgan Kingston, the famous operatic tenor, who went from a Mansfield coal mine to take a leading part at the Metropolitan Opera House, New York, has died at Stoke Poges.

Nottingham Journal 8th August 1936

During the last few years of his life Morgan Kingston returned to live in England. He died in a London Hospital in 1936 aged 61 and is buried at Stoke Poges Buckinghamshire.[14]

On Saturday May 15th 1999 ninety years after Alfred Webster (Morgan) Kingston sang at the opening of the Drill Hall in Forest Town, his melodic voice was once again heard in the building (now Kingsway Hall). This time however it was a group of enthusiasts playing one of his records as a tribute to this former singing miner.

NOTES

1 Kingston Genealogy in private hands.
2 William H Holland became well known in mining circles, he worked at Hucknall and Mansfield Colliery.
See Obituary, Mansfield Reporter 19 January 1934.
3 As above.
4 Printed article in untitled American publication, 7 January 1914.
5 Mansfield & North Notts. Advertiser 26 June 1908.
6 Mansfield & North Notts. Advertiser 21 May 1909.
7 Mansfield Reporter 7 Nov 1911.
8 Printed article in untitled American publication, 7 January 1914.
9 Kingston Genealogy in private hands.
10 As above.
11 As above.
12 As above.
13 Printed article in untitled American publication, 7 January 1914.
14 Kingston Genealogy in private hands.

17 - FOREST TOWN AND ROYALTY

The people involved with the negotiation and planning of Mansfield Colliery and the village of Forest Town, were born in the Victorian era. In 1900 when the initial work was taking place, Queen Victoria was still on the throne, however by the time the first houses were occupied there was a change of monarch. The queen had died on the 22 January 1901 after reigning for 63 years.

When the coronation of Edward the Seventh took place on 9th August 1902, it is not known if the residents of Sherwood Hall or the local farm tenants celebrated the occasion in any way. The Bolsover Colliery managers and their workers would have raised a glass to toast 'His Majesty', but at that time they did not have a Nottinghamshire colliery or village to warrant a local celebration.

This however was soon to change for it was during the reign of King Edward that Forest Town developed, and the first children of the new village were born. It was King Edward the children at Forest Town school would learn about. At school, each year Empire Day was an important occasion, and was always recorded in the school logbook.

> 25 May 1906 *'Empire Day' was celebrated today instead of on the 24th. Lessons upon the Empire were given during the morning and the schools closed in the afternoon.* [1]

However in May 1910 the usual celebration of this day had a more sombre note, for the entry reads:

> 24 May 1910 *'Empire Day' was celebrated today. Lessons upon the life of His late Majesty King Edward the Seventh were given during the morning, followed by the singing of suitable hymns and songs. The whole of the children were assembled and addressed in the playground before dismissal. In the afternoon the usual half day holiday was granted.* [2]

Just over one year later on the 11th June 1911 the school logbook recorded a happier celebration; '*the school closed at 4pm for a weeks holiday, in honour of the Coronation of His Majesty King George the Fifth.*'[3] For some of the school children recorded in the Forest Town School Admission Registers[4] this was the third monarch who had reigned in their short lives. Some of the children are listed below with their date of birth:

Hilda Mary Young	3rd March 1891	*John David Fox*	28th Aug. 1892
Ernest Cooke	22nd Jan. 1893	*Arthur Swain*	25th Sept. 1894
Thomas Murden	26th Sept. 1895	*Joseph Cutts*	3rd Oct. 1896
Issac Parkin	14th June 1897	*Arthur Vincent*	3rd April 1898
Leonard Toplis	28th Jan. 1898	*Hilda Selina Toplis*	21st Oct. 1899
Lily Gittings	20th Aug. 1900	*Leonard James Newton*	16th Oct. 1900

There were many more.

The new King George the Fifth was crowned at Westminster Abbey on the 22nd June 1911. Forest Town like many other places in the country celebrated this royal occasion. Local newspapers reported;

> *'In connection with the Coronation festivities 230 youngsters gathered on the Clipstone Road and made the 'Welkin Ring'[5] with the echoes of their patriotic song. A procession of children from tiny tots to sturdy youths was formed in the centre of the village and they sang enthusiastically 'Rule Britannia'. Afterwards the children aged 3-14 went to the Church of England and Non-conformist schools for tea and each child was given a medal. After tea they adjourned to some fields placed at disposal by Farmer Vincent where games and frolics indulged. Contests were organised and prizes to value of £5 were given. The Coronation Committee were Rev Bull, Mrs J. Guylor, J. Keeton, ?, Gunn and A. Gilliott, Representatives of the C. of E., Primitive and Wesleyan Methodists.[6]*

While the coronation of the new king and his queen were a time of great festivity for the people of the village, they were not aware then, that within three years they would once again have the opportunity to celebrate a very special royal event. In 1914 the local people really did rejoice when King George and Queen Mary came to visit the village of Forest Town.

The royal visit was part of a three day tour of Nottinghamshire, Derbyshire and Yorkshire which commenced on the 24th June 1914. As with all royal visits, the king and queen had a very tight schedule with various ceremonies to perform, and many people to meet. On the second day of the tour the arrangements for the visit to Forest Town were organised so that the royal party would arrive at the Forest Town Institute at 12:42pm, and remain for just 10 minutes.

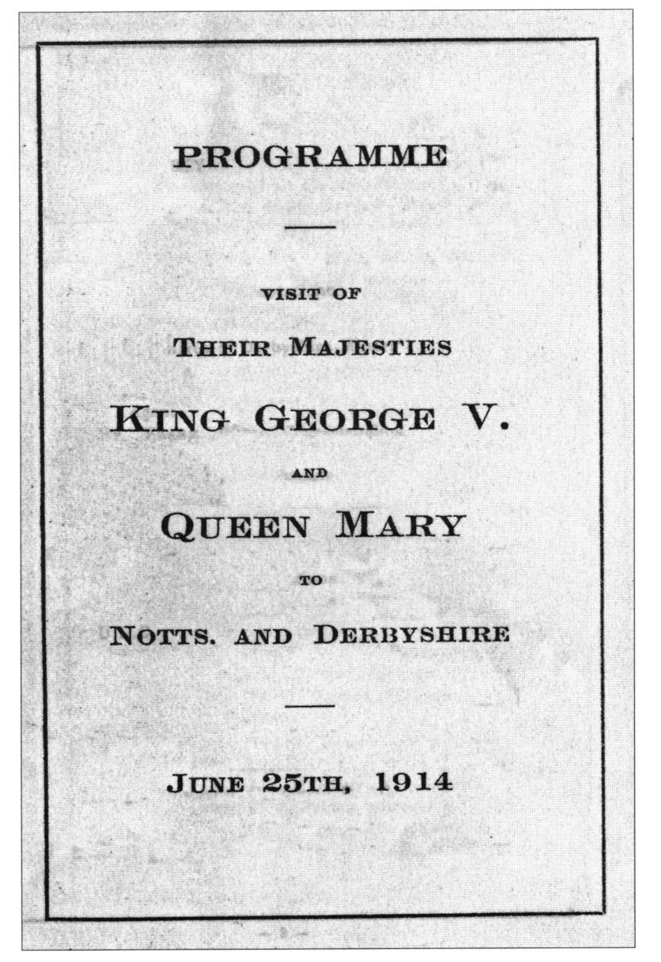
PROGRAMME

VISIT OF

THEIR MAJESTIES

KING GEORGE V.

AND

QUEEN MARY

TO

NOTTS. AND DERBYSHIRE

JUNE 25TH, 1914

Visit Crown Farm Colliery Village
Forest Town 12:42 12:52
Presentations at the Institute;
Directors of the Bolsover Colliery Company:
Mr. R. M. KNOWLES, Chairman of Directors.
Mr. J.P. HOUFTON, Managing Director.
Mr. W. H. CARTER, Manager of Colliery.
Notts. Miners' Association Representatives;
Mr. J.C. HANCOCK, M.P., Agent.
Mr. C. BUNFIELD, Secretary.
Mr. W. CARTER, Assistant Secretary,
Mr. L. SPENCER, Treasurer.

However on this occasion, the royal visit did not stick to the original plan, and the occasion turned out to be far more exciting than the local people could ever have imagined.

The weather on the 25th June was glorious, and after performing various official ceremonies in Mansfield, King George and Queen Mary travelled by car to Forest Town. The village was well prepared, as the Bolsover Colliery Company had spent a great deal of money on decorations to ensure their mining village was well presented.[7] As the royal car entered the village near St Alban's Church, an impressive sight met their eyes. A banner with the greeting

WELCOME TO THE KING & QUEEN

was stretched across the road, and the main street (Clipstone Road) was decorated with flags and bunting. The royal car slowed down to travel at 4 miles per hour, which would have delighted the hundreds of village people who lined the route. Two stands erected on either side of the school were crammed with tier upon tier of cheering flag waving children. A photograph that appeared in the Nottingham Guardian on the 27th June shows just how tightly packed the stands were.[8]

At the far end of the village on either side of the road, more stands had been erected, these were for members of the Primitive and Wesleyan Methodists, whose respective chapels stood opposite each other. After passing these stands of enthusiastic people, the royal cars turned right and drove under yet another banner which proclaimed "WELCOME" in letters 2' 6" (75mm) high. The banner had been painted on canvas, and two trellis type columns supported it, each was decorated with artificial red roses.

The cars then travelled past the Drill Hall, and houses in Second Avenue referred to as cottages in many of the newspapers;[9] on towards the Institute where official presentations were to take place. This road which has the houses of First Avenue on the right, and those of Second Avenue on the left, does not have the same garden facilities as the rest of the Avenues; it is said the road was specially widened for the royal visit,[10] and is now referred to as 'the wide backs.' Everywhere along the road, there were people cheering and waving flags. Many of them watched in amazement when the royal car stopped just before it reached the entrance to the Institute grounds; it had stopped in front of number 8 Second Avenue, the home of an ordinary working miner.

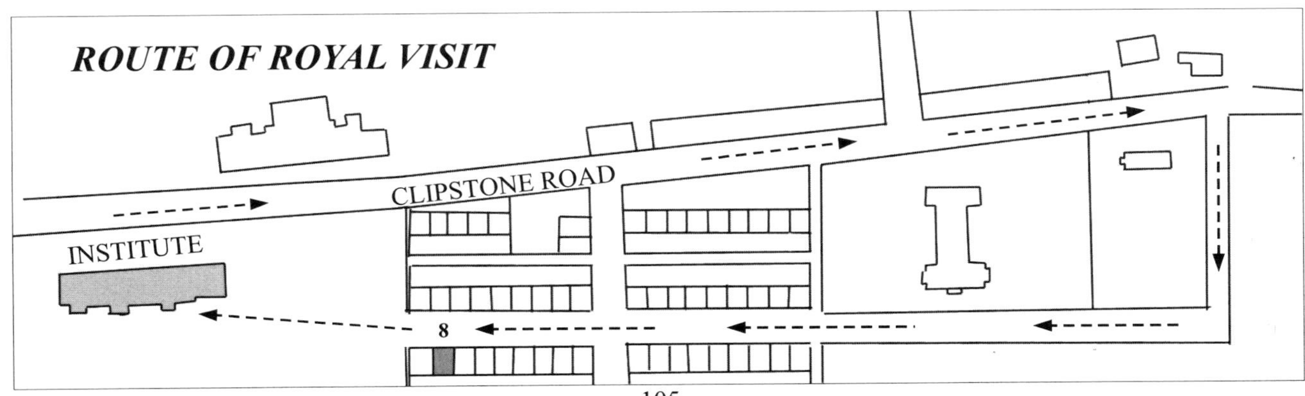

Elijah and Sarah Mottishaw

This was the home of Elijah and Sarah Mottishaw, and while it was rumoured the royal party were to visit a miner's cottage it is reasonable to assume that only a select few would have known that the Mottishaw's were to be the honoured family.

The King and Queen stepped out of their car and walked up to Elijah Mottishaw, a bearded man who stood at the door with his wife and daughter. The Queen is reported to have said, "We have come to see you, may we come in?"[11] It was said 'the couple were too surprised and delighted to respond in words but Mrs Mottishaw curtsied, and led the way into their cottage followed by the King, the Queen, and the Duke of Portland.'

They were shown into a well-furnished parlour and 'both the King and Queen complimented them on a fine harmonium,' (the Mottishaw's were reported to be a musical family).[12] By the window was a small table, this had ornamental china on it, and the Queen admiringly picked the china up piece by piece. Her Majesty then noticed a photograph on the mantelpiece and asked who it was; as Sarah Mottishaw was proudly explaining that the young man in the photograph was her son,[13] he entered the room and was introduced to the Queen.

The King was interested to discover more about the flag that he had noticed flying from the upstairs window of the house. Elijah Mottishaw told him that the flag came from Nanamimo, a mining camp in British Columbia, where he had once lived and worked. He had been in British Columbia ten years and two of his children had been born there. He eventually returned to England because of ill health.[14] Elijah now aged 56,[15] had been working at Mansfield Colliery for around eight years, and their Majesties discovered he was a 'Butty Miner' [16]

The royal visitors were also interested in seeing the kitchen, and this like the rest of the house was spotless. Here both the King and Queen were very interested in the painted mantelpiece,[17] which was said had been done by a crippled artist in the village. One newspaper described this interesting fireplace feature to be a landscape painting, however none of the newspapers gave the name of the talented local artist. There was not time to go upstairs and the royal party which also included the Duchess of Portland, and the Archbishop of York, eventually left the miner's cottage. As they stepped outside, they were once again greeted by cheers and waving flags.

Behind them, they left a family who not surprisingly soon found themselves the centre of much attention. The Mottishaw's who had lived in this house on the Avenues since 1906 must suddenly have become the most popular people on Second Avenue. Newspaper reporters and people in the village wanted to know every little detail of that very special royal visit.

The royal visitors leaving No 8 Second Avenue
(Photograph reproduced courtesy of the Evening Post)

The royal party after leaving No.8 Second Avenue, walked the short distance into the Institute grounds. This was possibly a new entrance, for the Nottingham Guardian newspaper refers to a road having been made through the grounds near the Institute for the royal visit.[18]

The Institute grounds and gardens were said to be 'looking their best.' [19] Both the balcony and pillars were festooned with real rambler roses. Richly emblazoned shields containing trophies of flags decorated the front of the building and six large flags flew from various parts of the roof.[20] A special platform covered in red baize had been erected in front of the Institute and the lovely Institute building adding a fitting background to the scene. To the front, the assembled party could look out on the lawns and playing fields of the Institute grounds.

The Institute grounds were the setting for the official and ceremonial part of the royal visit and over seven hundred men and boys in the employment of the Bolsover Colliery Company were on duty.

The uniforms of the Ambulance Brigade, Boys' Brigade, and Cadet Corps were being proudly worn. Some of the men and boys from the Bolsover and Creswell contingents had arrived at Forest Town by a special passenger train, and in doing so had created another 'first' for Forest Town. Their train was the first passenger train to travel on the new Mansfield Railway and as Forest Town did not have a station the train drew to a halt at the top of the pit approach road at around 11:15am.[21] From there the men and boys would have marched to take their place in the Institute grounds.

Officials being presented to the King and Queen at the Forest Town Institute
(Photograph reproduced courtesy of the Evening Post)

The Boys' Brigade formed the guard of honour, and under the command of Mr Carter gave the royal salute. The Duke of Portland then presented a number of specially selected people who were listed in the programme, (see page 104) to the king and queen. As befitted the occasion there were many other well known ladies and gentlemen present. Among these were:

Mr & Mrs J. P. Houfton,
Mr & Mrs R. L. Jones,
Mr & Mrs W. H. Carter
Mr & Mrs L. Spencer
Mr & Mrs Davis
Miss Agnes Houfton
Mr J. W. Houfton,
Mr & Mrs J. Bingley
Mr & Mrs C. Bunfield
Mr & Mrs J. G. Hancock
Mr & Mrs Wakefield

The wives of the colliery officials were also present.[22]

The official presentations were the climax of the royal visit to Forest Town, and once these were over the king and queen, preceded by the Duke of Portland returned to their cars. They left the village en route for lunch at Newstead Abbey with the loud cheers of an enthusiastic Forest Town community giving them a fitting send off.

The royal departure was not however the end of the festivities in the village. The Bolsover Colliery had provided for the Directors and other invited guests, a specially prepared lunch in the Institute. On the colliery football field, a marquee had been erected, where tea was provided for approximately 300 children and 600 members of the Boys' Brigade.

During the afternoon various sporting events took place, bowls between Mansfield Colliery and Worksop clubs, and a cricket match between the Mansfield and Bolsover Collieries. The children were also catered for with a programme of activities, punch and judy shows, fire balloons, and races in which each child entering received a prize to the value of 6^{d}.[23]

As a memento of this very special day, the Colliery Company gave each child a souvenir medal. The event has not been forgotten and over ninety years on (in 2005), the medals are still treasured.

NOTES

1 Forest Town School Logbooks in Private Hands..
2 As above.
3 As above.
4 Forest Town School Admission Register in Private Hands..
5 Welkin (means sky).
6 Mansfield Advertiser 23 June 1911.
7 Eyre & Sons of Chesterfield were contracted for much of this.
8 A news cutting of this photo has been found and is not suitable for reproduction.
9 The royal visit was reported in many local and national newspapers.
10 Sheffield Telegraph 25 June 1914, also oral history.
11 Yorkshire Herald 26 June 1914.
12 As above.
13 Daily Telegraph 26 June 1914.
14 As above, also Nottingham Express, and Nottingham Guardian 26 June 1914.
15 Yorkshire Herald 26 June 1914.
16 Nottingham Express 26 June 1914.
17 Daily Telegraph, and Nottingham Guardian 26 June 1914.
18 Nottingham Guardian 24 June 1914.
19 Sheffield Telegraph 25 June 1914.
20 Mansfield Chronicle 25 June 1914.
21 Mansfield & North Notts. Advertiser 26 June 1914..
22 As above.
23 As above.

18 - THE WAR YEARS

On the corner of 1st Avenue

In the days before television, radio, and very few telephones, it is difficult to imagine just how the news of the Great War of 1914-18 reached the people of Forest Town. However, newspapers were the real media in those days, and once alarming news had been read by a few, it would soon have spread round the village. Neighbours would have knocked on each other's doors, people would have congregated on street corners, and the miners would have heard the news as they left the pit. No one knew what such news meant for their community, they could only speculate.

As the Mansfield Colliery had developed, the population of Forest Town had risen. The new Mansfield Railway was in progress, and there were rumours that Forest Town would have a station.[1] It was also alleged that the war would only last a few months and would possibly be over by Christmas; a rumour that proved to be very wrong as Forest Town and communities throughout the land soon discovered.

Along with the rest of Britain, the people of Forest Town were asked to respond to the needs of the country. The poster declaring 'Your Country Needs You', was really aimed at encouraging young men to enlist and fight for king and country. The statement was to have far-reaching effects on the whole local community, not just the young male population of Forest Town.

In 1914, young men and boys of the Boys' Brigade and Cadets had already been introduced to a military regime of discipline and drill. They met in Drill Halls such as the one at Forest Town, which had been established by the Bolsover Colliery Company. These halls were recreational centres where many young people enjoyed sporting activities but where there was also an emphasis on discipline and drill. With the onset of war, for many of them the latter was soon to become a harsh reality.

The growth of Britain's army was initially dependent on enthusiastic volunteers, young men who were encouraged and praised from every quarter. An emphasis was placed on fighting not just for king and country, but for their town, county, work place, and even a soldier's family. It was something of which everyone could be proud. The death and the horror of war were not emphasised, that came later.

Those who declined the opportunity of such glory, risked being shunned by the local community. White feathers signified cowardice, and were given to those deemed as such. Advertisements in newspapers were aimed at the men who had so far declined to enlist. Equally the advertisements reflected on wives, children, families, and sweethearts of such men; did they really want a person in their lives who was not willing to fight in the war? Families had to face their neighbours; men had to face work colleagues and their employers. Pressure was everywhere.[2] None more so than in small mining communities.

A recruiting office was opened in Mansfield Town Hall, and by the end of August 300 men had joined the colours. Some of these men may well have been from Forest Town, as men from areas outside the town were encouraged to enlist at the Mansfield office. Departures of soldiers and some sailors were soon leaving Mansfield railway station.

The Duke of Portland from Welbeck Abbey, participated in recruiting campaigns, he urged all men to come forward and join the colours. An extra emphasis was placed on the importance of Nottinghamshire not falling behind other counties in recruitment.[3] The prestige of the county was a significant element of the war.

John P. Houfton was another person who played a notable part in many of the local recruiting campaigns.[4] He was well known and respected in the local coal industries, especially Mansfield (Crown Farm) Colliery and the people of Forest Town.

During the second week of September 1914, great scenes prevailed in the village where the focus of the excitement was the Drill Hall. At short notice, a meeting had been called, and the colliery band had paraded round the streets signalling the importance of the occasion and encouraging everyone to assemble at the Drill Hall. It was there that military personnel, colliery managers and local dignitaries joined John P. Houfton to speak to the local people. They stressed the urgency of recruiting for king and country, and emphasised joining the County Battalion of the Sherwood Foresters.[5]

Entrance to the Drill Hall

Many aspects of the war was fed to the people gathered in the Drill Hall that day. They heard how Germany had started the war, how Britain was keeping its word to Belgium, also of the cost and self-sacrifice by everyone as heroic young men enlisted.

John P. Houfton spoke of four meetings in Derbyshire he had attended the previous week. At those meetings a total of 750 men had been recruited, 'the bulk of whom were miners, men of whom the country might be proud'.[6] An occupation he stressed 'rendered them not only intelligent but made their muscles hard and rendered them fit for licking into shape to join the army abroad'.[7] The power of words was used to stir up the self-esteem of each miner present. Additionally the prestige of the Mansfield Colliery, and the people of Forest Town were also emphasised.

Everyone present was reminded that because of the recent visit by the king and queen,[8] and because of this Forest Town was now known all over England.

Miners from Forest Town worked at Mansfield Colliery, and 168 men from the colliery had already enlisted.

Those miners had left their wives, and their children behind. As an added encouragement, John P. Houfton said the Colliery Company would look after the men's dependants.[9]

Cheering accompanied the speeches and patriotic songs were sung with accompaniment from the colliery band. All of this added to the pressure placed on the young men present. Those who moved forward to give their name received loud acclaim. Many accolades were placed on young shoulders as they enlisted that day.[10]

On the 18th September 1914 a report in the Mansfield & Sutton Times was headed;

FOREST TOWN MEN ENLIST, BIG CROWDS SEE THEM OFF

It was a gallant band of fine strapping young fellows who left Mansfield on Monday to strengthen the Territorial Force. They came from Forest Town and marched through the town headed by a band. Hundreds of people had turned out to see them. First they had visited the Drill Hall and subsequently left by train for Newark. There was a tremendously big crowd at the station to give the men a cheery send off. The station officials doubted if there was ever a bigger crowd on the premises. At the head of the column Mr J. P. Houfton managing director of the Bolsover Colliery Company, marched accompanied by Major Sarll who went with the men to Newark. Before leaving the Drill Hall Mr Houfton and Rev. Harry Bull spoke a few words of encouragement to the recruits.[11]

The report continued by saying Mr Houfton addressed the recruits not as men but as English soldiers, who as such, would wherever they went behave themselves, and uphold the good name of British soldiers and Nottinghamshire miners. Additionally, Rev. Bull assured the men that Forest Town would never forget them.

A long list of names followed the report and included:

James Mace — *23 Sixth Avenue*
W. A. Davidson — *5 Fourth Avenue*
Geo. Wheatley — *34 Fourth Avenue*
Walter Moxon — *22 Fifth Avenue*

Ed. Mills	*20 Fourth Avenue*
G. Cutts	*4 Sixth Avenue*
C. A. Robottom	*14 Third Avenue*
E. Richardson	*32 Sixth Avenue*
L. Millard	*21 Eighth Avenue*
R. M Cooper	*11 Seventh Avenue*
J. T. Wardle	*2 Eighth Avenue*
T. Murden	*9 First Avenue*
G. Chester	*7 First Avenue*
Frank Boden	*31 Ninth Avenue*
E. Moxon	*9 Fourth Avenue*
C. Clarke	*2 Third Avenue*
C. A. Turner	*18 Fifth Avenue*
F. W. Ingham	*Sherwood Hall Cottages*

There were many more.

Publicity such as this was all part of the recruiting campaign. Headings such as *Mansfield and District Heroes* would include photographs and give brief information on the men, their regiment, their home address, and where the soldier had previously worked. For example the Mansfield Chronicle on Thursday 26th August 1915 featured

Pte William Houfton	*8th Batt. Sherwood Foresters*
Gunner William Naylor	*Royal Horse Artillery*
Pte J. O'Brien	*8th Batt. Sherwood Foresters*

all worked at Mansfield Colliery.

The local newspapers were important, they helped the community to share both the joys and sorrows of the war years and they kept them informed of new local developments that could have an effect on their lives.

For the people of Forest Town the war suddenly took on a new meaning. As hundreds of young men left the area to fight in distant lands, news that a large military training camp was to be built within a few miles of the village, suddenly became the topic of much speculation. The camp was Clipstone Camp, and within the space of a few months rows and rows of large wooden huts, with spaces for parade grounds and other facilities covered what was once open land. The building of the camp created many local concerns. Roads not built for heavy traffic were churned up, there was worry over sanitation, local water pollution and the spreading of infectious diseases.[12] There were many other worries about the welfare of the soldiers, also the women and children of the area.

The first soldiers arrived at Clipstone Camp in May 1915 and over the next few years thousands and thousands of them lived and trained there, moving on to fight in distant lands. The noise from soldiers boots rang out as they marched along the country lanes, often mixed with the sound of bugles playing. Shooting was heard from the rifle ranges, shouting as they lunged with bayonets and the noise of digging out trenches.[13]

One small section of Clipstone Camp, the camp that had a large impact on Forest Town, and the surrounding area.

Watching marching soldiers would have been fascinating for young people in the community. For some it would have brought an added awareness of their fathers, uncles and brothers who were fighting in the war.

An open day at the camp on the 13th July 1915, gave the opportunity for people from Forest Town and the wider community to satisfy their curiosity, and see what the military camp was really like. The population turned out in their thousands on a hot Sunday afternoon, they came from Mansfield, Alfreton, Bolsover, Blackwell, and Sutton, distances of up to sixteen miles. The road between Mansfield and the camp passed through Forest Town and it was congested with people on foot, in traps, wagons, and motorcars.[14] The air was thick with the sandy dust from the road surface, and everywhere there was the noise of people.

The open day at the camp offered light relief to the soldiers, they had added additional humour and huts displayed signs;

C View Apartments - To Let - Fortunes Told Here [15]

It added to the enjoyment of the visitors, and they could temporarily forget the fighting and news of death that was already reaching their communities. The people saw a place where soldiers could live, train, and have fun. The soldiers were like their own husbands, sons and employees who had recruited in the army, and they could warm to them. The open day at the camp was certainly a day to remember and people were amazed how large an area it covered.

There were times when the accommodation at the large camp was not sufficient, and 94 years old John Newton vividly recalled that while officers were billeted in Crown Farm where he was born and lived as a child, soldiers lived in tents in the

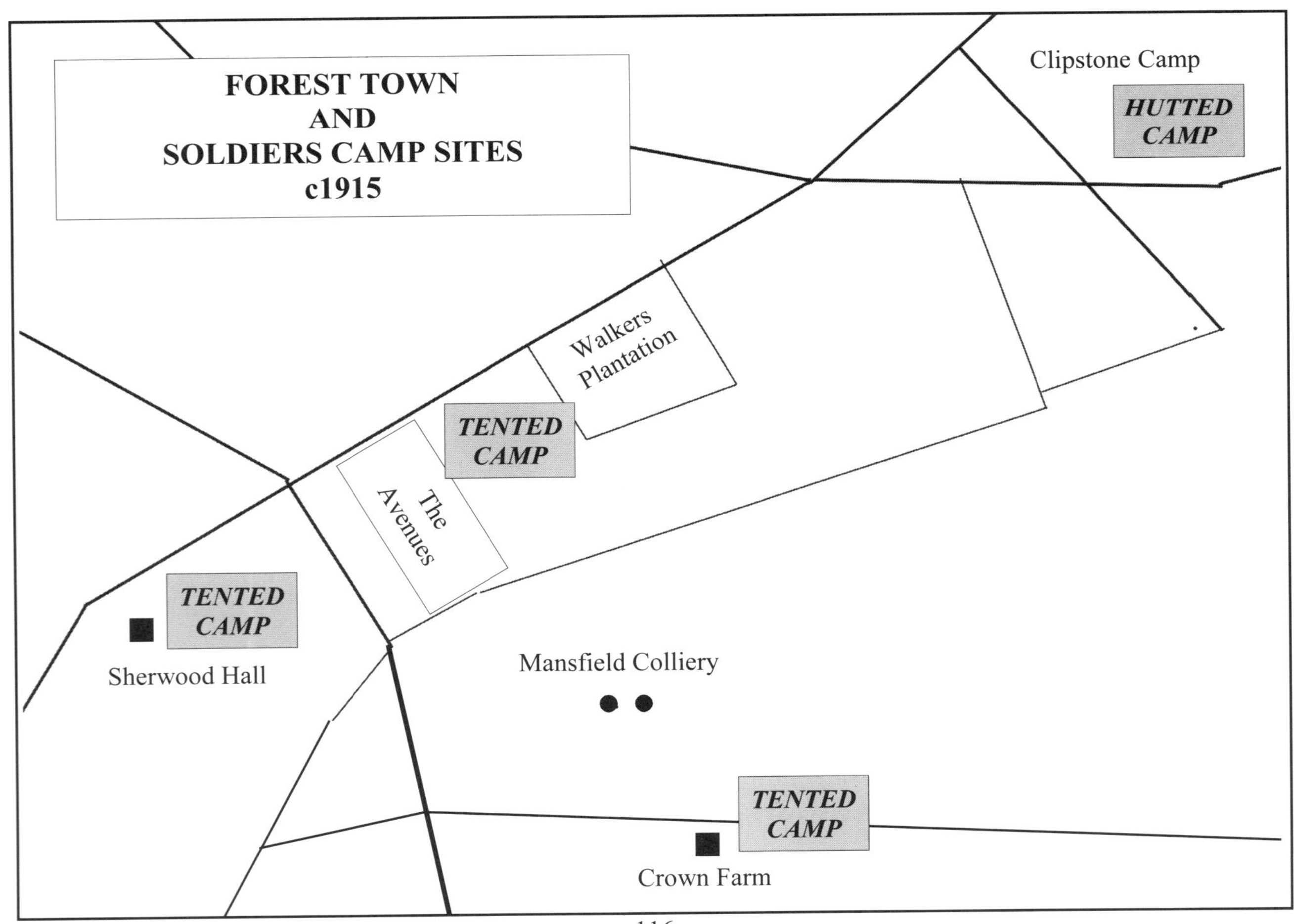

Soldiers camping in Walkers Plantation near to the Avenue houses.

paddock. In July 1915 newspapers reported that Royal Engineers were camped in tents at Sherwood Hall[16] and 2000 men camped in tents near Walkers Plantation on the Clipstone Road. The latter further added to the council's worries over sanitation, as these were near to the houses in Forest Town.[17]

It seems the soldiers and camps were something to write home about for in July 1915 a lady called Nellie who gave her address as 'care of 44 Clipstone Road, Forest Town' sent a postcard to her mother in Manchester, saying:

> *...Lovely weather here. There is a very large camp in the fields opposite our house - the Empire Battalion and we can see them drilling etc from the windows...*[18]

The presence of soldiers was everywhere, and this sometimes caused confusion for small children whose fathers had gone off to war. They would sit on fences watching the soldiers marching past and say to them 'we were waiting for our daddy.' [19]

Looking after the welfare of the soldiers was important; church and chapel people provided teas and refreshments at moderate prices, and they were invited into the homes of local people for tea.[20] Soldiers attended and participated in church services. Entertainment was provided for, and by the soldiers, and they participated in many local fund raising concerts.

FOREST TOWN

A concert in the Primitive Methodist School Room Forest Town was given to a large audience by men from Clipstone Camp known as ***The Glad Idlers RAMC***.

Among the entertainers were
Pte Harwood - The Humorist
Pte Aichman & Pte Clegg - Light Comedian

[other names given]

Extract from Mansfield Chronicle
6 April 1916

Soldiers were invited to use the Forest Town Institute with its tennis courts, bowling green, and sports ground. The sports ground was a popular venue for events. "Varsity Cricket" was a first class attraction in June 1915. Officers and NCO's of the UPS [University & Public Schools] Brigade, some who had made their name playing for counties such as Cambridge, Oxford, Middlesex and Sussex competed. The proceeds from the event raised £5 for the Red Cross. Another match between Mansfield Colliery and the Royal Fusiliers took place later that month.[21] Military sports on the Institute ground were of a special attraction to the civilian population and were unusual to say the least as they included grenade throwing and sandbag filling competitions.[22]

GRAND CRICKET MATCH
MANSFIELD COLLIERY
v
98TH BRIGADE (Royal Fusiliers)
ON SATURDAY JUNE 26TH
on the
FOREST TOWN GROUND
Wickets pitched at 11.30am
Teams to be selected from the following:-

Mansfield Colliery	**Royal Fusiliers**
J. White	J. C. Hartley Oxford Un. & Sussex.
A. Warren	M. W. Payne, Cambridge & Middx.
T. Poole	N. J. Holloway, Cambridge & Sussex.
C. Chester	C. E. Lucas, Cambridge & Sussex.
J. Barnes	C. P. Arnold, Cambridge & Hamps.
W. Cooper	R. C. Cutter, Cambridge & Roxsall.
W Whysall	C. H. Skey, Cambridge & Queens Coll.
O. Wass	N. Miller, Dulwich & Surrey.
W. Davis	H. W. Ling, Old Roswallians.
A.Saxton	G. Jones, Cheshire.
J. Purdy	Capt. Holland.
T. S____	A. Black
W. Smith	A. C. Saville

Entrance fee 3d each. Soldiers and ladies free

Mansfield Chronicle 24th June 1915

There could be 20 to 30,000 soldiers stationed at the camp at any one time, and such vast numbers gave the opportunities for additional local trade. Soldiers who walked through Forest Town on their way to Mansfield had the opportunity to use the village shops that could supply many of their basic needs. Local postcards were a popular item and some with their messages have survived today, such as the one of St Alban's Church posted in July 1916 to Miss P. Hunt, The Ridgeway, Golders Green, London:

> *Dear Phil, We pass this church on our way to Mansfield, it is about 1½ miles from the camp...it is raining as usual.*
>
> *Good bye, Love to all, Harold*

Young boys from the village delivered newspapers to the camp and local families who though often short of house space, managed to find room to take in soldiers' families for short visits,[23] the prospect of a little added income was always welcome.[24]

Local people such as Shadrach Osler,[25] J T Goodman, J. H. Raybould and T. G. Swift,[26] started taxi and omnibus businesses to take soldiers to and from the camp. The local council was kept busy with applications for the appropriate licenses, and petrol storage. The traffic through the village increased and Forest Town was not quiet throughout the war. In October 1917, the Mansfield Railway finally opened a passenger service to the camp.[27] While this would have reduced some of the traffic on the roads, Forest Town would still have been a busy place.

Montague Osler is stood at the front of his taxi. The men may be civilian workers at the camp? The huts of Clipstone Camp are in the background

There was, of course, a more sombre side to the war for the local community. By mid December 1914 the village of Forest Town was in mourning, and the first memorial plaque of the war was unveiled in St. Alban's Church. This was to Corporal F. J. Munnings of the Kings Own Yorkshire Light Infantry [KOYLI], a former choirboy at the church, and one of the first of 362 men from Mansfield Colliery who had 'answered their country's call.' Corporal Munnings aged 31 of Eighth Avenue Forest Town, had been killed in France and was buried in Boulogne.[28] His wife and three children were left with their memories.

In Memory of
Corporal F. J. Munnings,
of the
2nd Batt. KOYLI
Who was wounded in the service
of his Country
And Died at Boulogne, France
on Nov. 15th 1914
He was a Chorister of this Church
And a Respected Officer of the
Forest Town Boy's Brigade
By whom this tablet was erected.

Over the next few years, many other Forest Town people were to learn of the death of a member of their family, or men who had worked at Mansfield Colliery, been members of their church, and of other colleagues. They also endured the sadness of watching the military funerals of 26 soldiers and one nurse from Clipstone Camp; deaths which occurred from accidents, influenza, bronchitis and pneumonia.[29] Simple crosses which originally marked each grave were first dedicated in July 1917.[30] In later years they were replaced to the standard commonwealth war grave headstone.

Local children were not immune to the horror of war; the patriotism of military

A military funeral in St Alban's churchyard. Sergt. Orridge RE is hand written on the back of the postcard.

Note the Forest Town Institute can be seen in the background.

funerals was instilled into the children of the Forest Town School, which was adjacent to the churchyard. The children and their teachers remained silent as they heard the gun carriage go past, the graveside gun salute, and the bugle playing the last post.[31] In the churchyard, local people joined soldiers from the camp. The war and death united the community and they paid tribute together.

Not surprisingly a number of long term relationships developed because of the camp, and some were married at St Alban's Church, Forest Town. Not all arose from friendships with local girls for the Registers show marriages between soldiers and WAACs. who both gave their address as Clipstone Camp.[32] WAACs were stationed at the camp towards the end of the war. In the Baptism Registers of St Alban's [33] and the Methodist Church[34] the child's father was often given as 'soldier'. Whether those soldier fathers were present to see their child baptised is unknown.

Life went on for the community of Forest Town. In the school Mrs Titchener, a teacher was absent in September 1917 for a day, as her husband had received orders for service in France.[35] In January 1918 the school was closed to enable staff to assist with the issuing of ration cards.[36] On the afternoons of 24th and 27th September 1918 the school was closed so that schoolchildren could go blackberry picking, they picked over 83 lbs.[37] which was a great achievement. The subsequent use made of this fruit would have been a valuable asset in times of food rationing. A special half-day holiday was granted on the 12th November 1918 in honour of the declaration of the armistice.

The armistice celebrations came only a few weeks after the village community had gathered at St Alban's Church for the unveiling of a Roll of Honour. The inscribed Roll listed the names of those from Forest Town who had been killed in the war; it formed the centre of a trophy of the flags of the allies, ornamented with flowers and laurels. Soldiers and buglers from Clipstone Camp, along with a very large congregation listened to Rev. Bull as he spoke of the men and boys who had once been choir-men, Sunday School teachers, communicants and members of the congregation.[38] It was a moving time for all those present.

Unveiling of the Roll of Honour at St Alban's Church Sunday 29th September 1918

At the beginning of July 1919, a local newspaper report stated 'peace was celebrated with full honours at Forest Town.' Once again the village was the scene of a large procession led by the colliery band, followed by all the children, the Boys' Brigade and Cadets. Then came special constables and demobilised soldiers and sailors who had turned out in full force. The parade ended on the Institute grounds where many people had assembled to greet them, and to participate in a united service. Rev. Bull (St Alban's Church), Mr A. Shaw (Primitive Methodists) and Mr G. Lee (Wesleyan Methodists) took part along with united choirs. The colliery band played before and after the service. The celebrations continued in the afternoon with a musical service arranged in St Alban's Church by the St Alban's Men's Class. There were many recitals and recitations. In the evening a special service was conducted by Rev. Bull and the Te deum was sung. This was followed by an organ recital played by Sergt. W. Brown LTC Lond., of the Queens Regiment.[39]

The Peace celebrations continued in Forest Town when the village entertained its own discharged and demobilised soldiers to a 'welcome home' tea in the Drill Hall. Wives and friends had also been invited and around 300 people were present. Mr & Mrs Daxon and their daughter Phyllis from the Welfare Institute, did the catering and local ladies served at the tables. Mr W. H. Carter chairman of the committee who had organised the event paid tribute to the soldiers. While he expressed joy at seeing them all again, he also said 'I cannot help feeling great sorrow as I look round at the wife, the mother, and the thoughts of the little ones, whose loved one is absent today, he who will never return.' [40]

Mr Carter additionally paid tribute to the workmen at the colliery, declaring that 'no colliery in the country had done more for its soldiers and sailors than Mansfield Colliery. Each year of the war had seen over one million tons raised.' He continued to speak on the state of the industry at the present time before asking the newly appointed manager of the Bolsover Colliery, Mr Albert Davis to make two presentations of medals relevant to the occasion. These were the DCM, awarded to Lance-corporal W. E. Boot of the RE, and Corporal J. Webster of the RAMC. Corporal Webster had been one of the first boys to enlist as a soldier in August 1914.[41]

Three years later in September 1921, a tall granite War Memorial was unveiled in St Alban's churchyard. Once again this was an occasion for all the community to take part in, as none were untouched by the war.

The Mansfield and North Notts. Advertiser on the 30th August 1921 told its readers:

> *The Drill Hall was made the gathering ground and there under the guidance of Mr W. H. Carter, captain of the local company of the Boys' Brigade, assisted by Mr Charles Lacey, secretary to the company, a procession was arranged. First came Forest Town Silver Band, then a military guard of four men from Mansfield who were to take charge of the cross during the service and subsequent unveiling. Forest Town British Legion, Boys' Brigade with Ambulance and Bugle Band, representatives from Mansfield Woodhouse Urban District Council, a party carrying wreaths, and the general public. The procession had not far to walk from the Drill Hall to the church, but it increased considerably en route.*

After a packed service in St Alban's Church everyone moved outside for the unveiling ceremony. The tall granite cross was draped with a Union Jack. At the four corners stood a soldier from the Notts. and Derbyshire Regiment, each with his head bowed and arms reversed. A specially erected stand had been erected for children from all the Sunday Schools in the village. All around in the churchyard and on the road, stood the clergy, the choir, local dignitaries and the village community.

They watched as Mr John Plowright Houfton unveiled the memorial and Rev H. Bull dedicated the Cross saying;

In the name of the Father and of the Son, and the Holy Ghost we dedicate this memorial to the Glory of God in memory of

G. Bradshaw	*G. Bullock*
J. E. Burton	*F. Carter*
N. Chadbourne	*W. Garton*
W. Heald	*J. Kelk*
S. Lancashire	*A. Lee*
F. Monks	*W. Moxon*
F. J. Munnings	*J. T. Murden*
A. Peatman	*S. F. Pickering*
E. Richardson	*W. Sheldon*
I. Taylor	*F. Thompson*
J. Thorpe	*F. H. Wilkinson*
H. Wilson	

The wreaths that were laid then, and are still laid at the beautiful carved granite memorial each November are a lasting tribute not only to those brave men, but to the Forest Town community during the years of the Great War.[42]

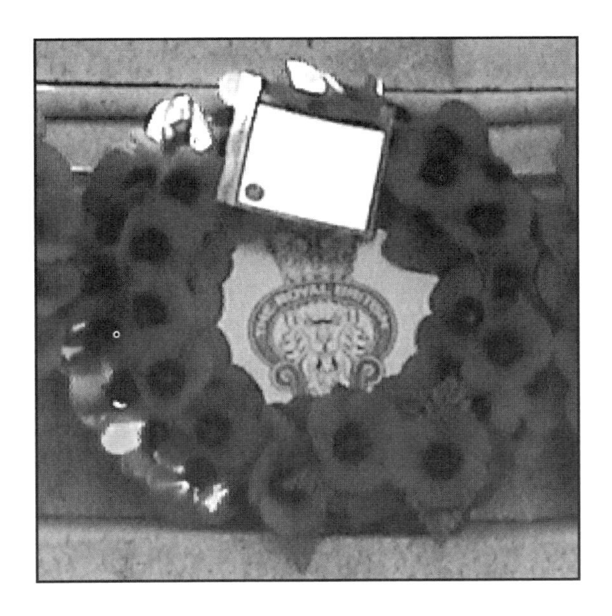

NOTES

1. This never did materialise.
2. Author's MA Dissertation Nottingham 1997.
3. As above.
4. John P. Houfton, appointed Manager and Secretary of Bolsover Colliery Company January 1890, General Manager 1897, Director 1910, retained a seat on the Board until his death in November 1929.
5. Mansfield Reporter, 11 September 1914.
6. As above.
7. As above.
8. King George and Queen Mary touring Nottinghamshire in June 1914 visited Forest Town, where at their request they entered a coal miner's house and chatted to the occupants.
9. Mansfield Reporter, 11 September 1914.
10. Author's MA Dissertation Nottingham 1997.
11. Mansfield & Sutton Times 18 September 1914.
12. Mansfield & Sutton Times 31 December 1914.
13. Remains of trenches can still be discovered in Sherwood Pines Forest at Clipstone.
14. Mansfield Chronicle 27 June 1915.
15. As above.
16. Mansfield Chronicle 15 July 1915.
17. NA DC/M/1/3/4/6 26 July 1915 & 27 September 1915.
18. Private postcard collection.
19. Oral history Phyllis Newton (nee Vamplew) now aged 92.
20. Oral histories, Mrs Staley, Rhoda Cope, Ken Nicholson.
21. Mansfield Chronicle, 10 June 1915.
22. Mansfield Chronicle, 15 June 1916.
23. Oral histories, various.
24. Mansfield Chronicle, 10 June 1915.
25. Shadrach Osler had the first Post Office in Forest Town.
26. NA DC/M 1/1/23.
27. PRO. Rail 468/11.
28. Mansfield Reporter, 18 December 1914.
29. St Alban's Burial Register. Photocopy in Private Collection, the original has now been deposited in N.A.O.
30. Mansfield & North Notts Advertiser 6 July 1917.
31. Oral histories, John Newton, Mrs Staley.
32. NA PR 21/122.
33. NA PR 21/119.
34. In private hands.
35. School Logbook in private hands.
36. As above.
37. As above.
38. Mansfield Chronicle 3 Oct 1918.
39. Mansfield & North Notts. 11 July 1919.
40. Mansfield & North Notts. Advertiser 8th Aug 1919.
41. As above.
42. For the purpose of this book only WW1 is mentioned; the names of men who died in WW2 are also on the memorial and are duly remembered each year.

19 - PEOPLE AND EVENTS

The Mansfield Colliery was the crucial link between the growth of the village and the binding together of the community. The prospect of work at this new colliery encouraged miners and their families to move from established communities such as Hucknall, Kirkby Woodhouse, Creswell, Shirebrook, and Whitwell. They came from many counties such as Derbyshire, Leicestershire, Staffordshire, Yorkshire, and elsewhere. The prospect of long term employment at a new colliery, plus good quality housing and the reputation of the Bolsover Colliery Company, was the incentive to move to the new Nottinghamshire village of Forest Town.

There were soon many extended families living in the nine Avenues of Forest Town's first housing estate. Relatives were encouraged by what they heard, and they followed other members of their family to live here. They brought with them sporting and musical talents; others had organising ability, and many were keen to establish their religious beliefs. They were the pioneers that helped the new community to grow.

Working at the colliery was the main occupation of the men and boys who lived in the village. It was the way of life of fathers, sons, uncles, and brothers, who worked at the coal mine that became known as *Crown Farm* or *Crownie*. In the early days many young boys such as the ones listed below, left Forest Town School and were employed at the colliery.

NAME	BORN	ADDRESS	LEFT SCHOOL	STARTED WORK DOWN PIT
Midwinter Frank	12. 1. 1906	21 Second Ave	7. 2. 1919	18. 8. 1920
Ratcliffe John T.	14. 5. 1906	15 Ninth Ave	30. 6. 1919	18. 8. 1920
Purdy John F.	3. 6. 1906	7 Ninth Ave	30. 6. 1919	18. 8. 1920
Woolley Peter	19. 5. 1906	23 Eighth Ave	30. 6. 1919	20. 7. 1920
Edgington Stanley	17. 4. 1906	24 Fifth Ave	25. 7. 1919	18. 8. 1920

Compiled from School Admission Registers and Records held at Derbyshire Record Office

Coupled with this were the associated activities that were key factors in the local community; the Boys' Brigade, Cadets, and St John's Ambulance Brigade. The knowledge of first aid was an asset in the hazardous mining industry. The Bolsover Colliery Company encouraged membership and participation in all these groups, people were proud to belong to them. The village community took pleasure in the success and achievements of their fellow men. They enjoyed seeing them in their respective uniforms, and delighted in the trophies and medals that were won, especially those of the colliery bands.

Associations such as the National Friendly Society were established in the village from 1905. Friendly Societies were a form of mutual insurance club and could offer families help in times of need. The societies had both a social and official side. In

October 1907 its first annual tea was held in the Primitive Methodist schoolroom, 170 members and friends attended. During the speeches, the divisional secretary for Nottinghamshire said that Forest Town district was one of his best young districts, and complimented Mr W. Sanderson, the secretary on all he had achieved to make it so. Entertainment followed with the Forest Town String Band making its debut, the conductor was Mr J. Cupit. Among the soloists were Miss Lizzie Shooter, and Mr E. R. Morris. Frank Bevise was said to have brought the house down with his humorous sketches while Mr J. Albon was well received with his "Queen of Angels." Members J. Banner, J. Hopewell and J. W. Hamilton also contributed to the entertainment and Mr H. Davis was said to be an able accompanist.[1]

From 1905 enthusiastic allotment holders and gardeners could join the Horticultural Society in Forest Town and were encouraged to participate in regular events. In August 1907 the second Annual Exhibition was held on the Forest Town cricket ground. This was divided into two classes, one for the cottagers (sic) employed at Mansfield Colliery, and the one for anyone who paid an entrance fee of five shillings to the society. The event was staged in large marquees and the categories included allotment gardens, cage birds, and for the children drawing, handwriting, kites and baskets of wild flowers. The prize winners were;

New Allotments
1 - *C. Price* 2 - *J. Bowen* 3 - *T. Annable* 4 - *H. Cook*

Old Allotments
1 - *W. Bingham* 2 - *J. Annable* 3 - *J. Bullock* 4 - *C. Hepton*

The judges of the horticultural section were gardeners from some of the larger houses in the area: Messrs A. Wragg *(at Osslington Hall),* F. Oliver *(Berry Hill),* T. Stubbing *(Sherwood Hall).* There were additional activities to encourage people to go to the event such as athletic sports races, and music by the band of the Queens Own Yorkshire Dragoon Guards.[2]

Forest Town festivities

The photograph which is believed to be of that event in August 1907 shows just how exciting the occasion would have been for the whole village. It would have been appropriate to send the picture to someone who may even have attended that Horticultural Exhibition in Forest Town such as Captain Tomlinson who was at St David's Mission Church during 1907. Little is known of him or how long he was at the Mission Church but he had obviously made friends with the Toplis family who lived at 27 First Avenue, Forest Town. They sent him the picture on a postcard dated the 3rd October 1908, it read:

to *Captain Tomlinson, The Homestead, Mount Durran, Guernsey.*

We should very much like to spend a holiday with you
as we have got a week now.
Father and mother and all of us send our love to you.

Hilda and H. & L. Toplis

The horticultural events created a great deal of interest from both competitors and sponsors. A surviving 1909 programme reveals there were 80 different categories of entries each with a 1st, 2nd and 3rd prize of money. There was also over 38 special prizes such as;

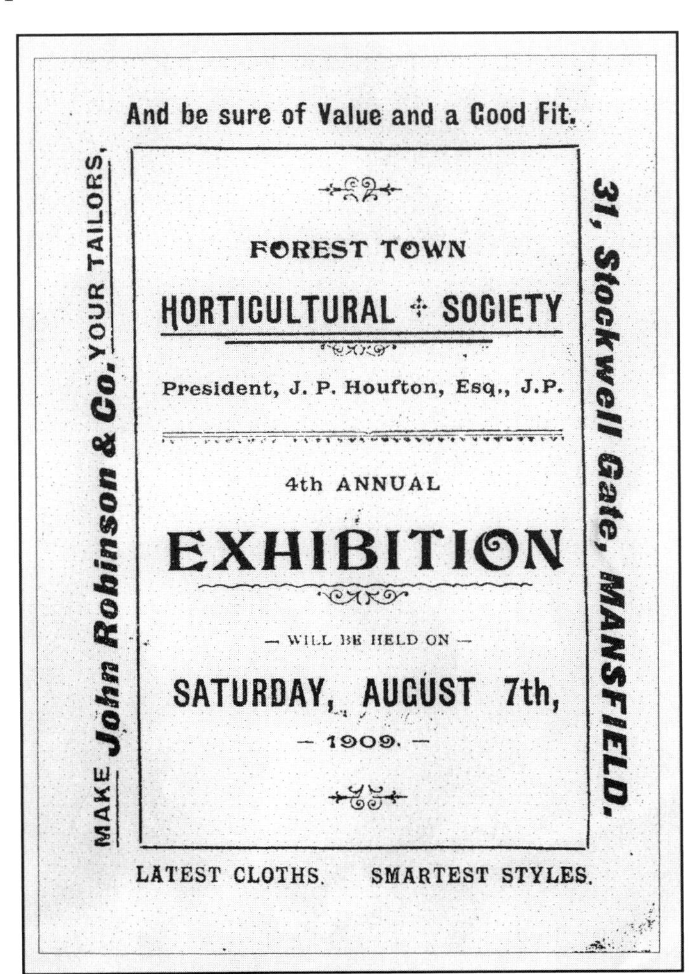

Mr Joe Bingley will give

First prize	*4 shillings [20p]*
Second prize	*3 shillings [15p]*
Third prize	*2 shillings [10p]*
Fourth prize	*1 shilling [5p]*

for best arranged basket of wild flowers open to children of employees of Mansfield Colliery and attending a day school.

The Bolsover Colliery Company Ltd gave wheelbarrows to the winners of the best cultivated old allotment, and best cultivated new allotment in Forest Town.

Mr Bainbridge of Sherwood Hall, offered money prizes for the best flower garden in the village facing north, and for the one facing south. Businesses in Mansfield and surrounding area gave prizes of money, cigars, whisky, port, brandy, steel spade, wicker chair, copper kettle, and pork pie, etc. A Brass Band contest also added to the competitiveness of the day.[3]

In this coal mining village when more is heard about the male members of the community, it has to be remembered that women also played a valid role in local life. They coped in an era when there wasn't any of the labour saving equipment we know today, nor modern sanitation. The women kept their houses clean, and swept their yards as befitted the tenancy agreement. They would cook, sew, and take in washing or lodgers if times were hard.

Young girls left school, helped their mothers, and found occupations to help with the family income. In its first few years the village school had many women teachers, among them were:

Mrs Kate Rudge, Miss Florence Bodell, Miss Adeline Frost,
Miss Elizabeth Shooter, Miss Mabel Silverton Stafford,
Miss Doris Barbara Sarll, Miss Carrie Agnes Poole.[4]

Margaret Bull, wife of Rev Bull, was noted for her work in the village, and her sewing classes for women and young girls.[5] The ladies worked hard making things for many fund raising events that helped to build and furnish the churches and chapels in Forest Town. Rev Harry Bull opened one active ladies group, the Mothers Union, on the 22nd December 1913. It is believed to have started with the following members;

Mrs Elizabeth Saunderson, Mrs Ann Roberts,
Mrs or Miss's, Bingley, Wakefield, Davis, S. Hargreaves,
E. Hargreaves, S. Annable, C. Swaby, Boden and Thorne.

From that first meeting, the Mothers Union in Forest Town continued to grow and be a very active association well into the 1960's, possibly even later.[6]

The young girls of the village were also catered for when the Girls' Brigade was started in the 1920's, if not before. They were proud of their 'Lincoln Green' tunics with red braid girdles, the red girdle was the colour of the Mansfield Colliery Girls' Brigade.

With concerts, plays, groups, religious services and many sporting activities the people of Forest Town had plenty to fill their lives with. The newspapers were keen to report events of all description, and they reveal the names of many local people, events and groups connected to the village and Mansfield Colliery.

30th March 1906 *A bazaar in aid of the debt on the Primitive Methodist school-chapel, was opened on Saturday, by Councillor Singleton, Mayor of Mansfield. Those in charge of stalls were:- Drapery, Mrs Jennings, Mrs Robinson, Mrs Gumm and Miss Annable. Fancy Goods, Miss Sayles, Miss Parkinson, Mrs Annable, Miss N. Bingham and Mrs Sayles. Flowers, Mrs Scott and Miss Wilson. Refreshments Mrs Smith, Mrs Hamilton, Mrs Wood, Mrs Share and Mrs Slack. Ice cream, Miss Bingham and Miss Redfern. Bran tub, Mr J. Redfern.*[7]

12th June 1908 *Mansfield Colliery Cricket. Warsop & Mansfield Colliery played at Warsop*[8]

Mansfield Colliery Players					
G. Smith	b	T. White			6
W. Davis	b	T. White			27
F. Taylor	c	Blackburn	b	Edwards	21
A. Boot	b	E. Morris			1
W. Cook	c	H. Riley	b	Morris	0
J. Taylor	b	Morris			5
H. Eames	b	Horan			0
G. Kemp	b	Horan			4
A. Tebbett	st	H. Riley b Edwards			6
J. Hart		not out			7
H. Davis	c	H. Riley	b	Morris	9
Extras					16
					102

11th September 1908 *There was a large gathering on the cricket ground on Sunday for a very enjoyable vocal and instrumental concert given by the Mansfield Colliery Orchestral Band, Silver Prize Band, and Choral Society in aid of funds for the Mansfield Hospital... Prior to the concert the Silver Prize Band paraded Big Barn Lane, Carter Lane and Forest Town. Speakers at the event were Rev H. Bull and Councillor W. Carter JP. Among the musical items was a solo by A .W. Kingston.*[9]

5th March 1909 *Concert - Bible Class & Christian Endeavour, in connection with Primitive Methodists Church gave a concert on Friday. Mr A. Bircumshaw presided, and there was a crowded audience. Programme of part songs & part choir. Songs - duets: Messrs Stanley & Bode; Recitations - Misses Taylor & Bingham, & Mr Bonser, Song Miss Gittings; quartet, members of the CE; Comic Songs Mr W. Taylor, a laughable sketch caused great amusement.*[10]

20th November 1914 *A report on 'Mayoral Sunday' tells of how 'a big contingent came swinging along from Forest Town (to Mansfield Market Square) led by the Colliery Prize Band, playing a patriotic air. Men and boys marched well and were quite a feature of the procession.' When all the civic dignitaries and various other units such as Police, Fire Brigade, Boy Scouts, Mansfield Military Band and the Old Comrades Association arrived the procession was formed up. In the lead was the Mansfield Colliery Silver Prize Band, Mansfield Colliery Bugle Band, Mansfield Colliery Boys' Brigade and Mansfield Colliery Ambulance Division.*[11]

29th June 1916 *The Patronal Festival in connection with St Alban's Church has been held this week, and on Saturday last the school children, to the number of about 300, had their annual treat. They had tea in the Parish Hall, and then went to a field kindly lent by Mr Vincent for games. On Sunday there were services at the church when the vicar Rev H. Bull preached appropriate sermons to good congregations.*[12]

An early photograph of Mansfield Colliery Cricket Team taken outside the club hut on the Institute ground

There were many activities and events encouraging people to socialise, but as with all communities, Forest Town was not without its tragic events. Events that then, as today would touch the hearts of the local people.

In October 1906 four year old Alvin Tebbett died after his flannelette nightshirt caught fire. His mother who was outside, saw the child through the window and could not get in as the door catch had fastened on the inside. A neighbour Mr Roe was able to break a window and helped Mrs Tebbett to look after the child until Doctor Houfton arrived. The youngster was very badly burned and did not survive.[13]

In January 1908 young Edwin Wroe died in Mansfield Hospital after he was badly burnt at his Forest Town home. At the inquest his parents told of how there was a fire in the wash house and the little boy was playing marbles there. It was believed that his clothes had caught when he had tried to get a marble that had rolled under the grate. When he ran screaming into the yard, his father Arthur Wroe, assistant manager of Crown Farm Colliery grabbed him and put the flames out. He took him to the hospital but sadly the young boy died.[14]

Christmas 1908 was a time William Haslam and family who lived in Sixth Avenue would never forget. They had gone to visit friends in Hucknall and their 8 week old daughter Elizabeth Anne shared their bed and during Christmas Night died from suffocation.[15]

In a close knit mining community news of an accident at the Mansfield Colliery would soon spread round the village. In September 1906, Fred Annable of Forest Town, and John Patrick of Mansfield were seriously injured when the cage in which they were descending dropped too quickly. Another Forest Town man, G. Jessop also received bruising to his legs.[16]

George Perry, colliery carpenter of Forest Town was called to give evidence at an inquest in May 1908, after George Powell a colliery day man of Sandy Lane, Mansfield, died when he fell 74 feet [22.6m] down the pit shaft. He left a widow with five children.[17]

The war years additionally brought their sorrows with the death of young men fighting for king and country, Frederick James Munnings (31) died November 1914,[18] Ernest Richardson (20) died August 1915,[19] Walter Moxon (28) died June 1917, Harry Wilson (29) died July 1918, Simeon Lancashire (19) died September 1918,[20] and there were many more. The village people were united in their grief.

Despite the times of sorrow there was also opportunities for rejoicing in happy family occasions. At the beginning of December 1918 St Alban's Church was licensed for marriages and the newspapers were soon telling readers;

> **12th December 1918** *'A Pretty Wedding At Forest Town' tells of the first wedding to be solemnised at the St Alban's Church. The couple to have this honour, and to make history at the church were Mr Reginald Wragge Morley, eldest son of Mr & Mrs Morley of Reading, and Miss Nellie Davis eldest daughter of Mr & Mrs Davis of Forest Town.*
>
> *The Bestman was Captain Weir, Chaplain to the forces at Clipstone. The bridesmaids were Miss Mollie and Miss Lena Davis (bride's sisters) and Misses Hudson and Westwick. Rev H. Bull curate-in-charge at St Alban's was assisted by the Rector of Lockwood Huddersfield Rev Hayden Gowe MA. Mr H. Toplis was the organist. Among the gifts was a silver tea service from underground officials and friends at Crown Farm Colliery.*[21]

In the ensuing years other weddings followed, and for many couples the service would have been followed by a 'tea' at the home of one of their parents, and if they were lucky a photograph was taken in front of the house. However one couple, Phyllis Mary Daxon, and Sydney Herbert Bacon, were a little more fortunate.

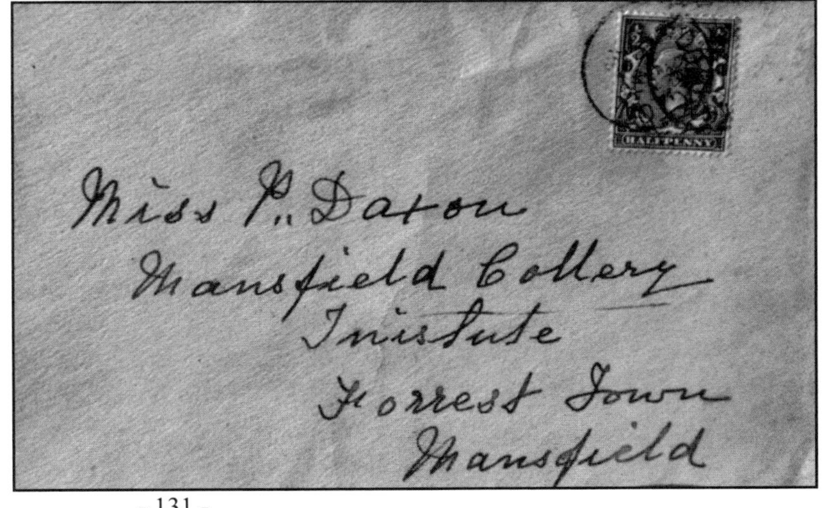

6th September 1921
After the marriage of Sydney Herbert Bacon and Phyllis Mary Daxon photograph taken outside the Mansfield Colliery Institute.

They were married at St Alban's Church on the 6th September 1921, and had a reception for 140 guests at the Miners' Institute where the bride's parents were the steward and stewardess. The wedding warranted a big report in the local newspaper that carried a list of the guests, and the gifts they gave to the happy couple. This included a tray, tea service and spirit kettle from the committee and members of Mansfield Colliery Institute. A climax to the day for the local people would have been watching the newlyweds leave in a motor car for their honeymoon in Skegness.[22]

While there are many family names remembered from the early days of Forest Town, one of the first notable ones was the Houfton family, who though they did not live in Forest Town, were often to be seen at many village events.

Arthur Frederick Houfton built a number of the properties in Forest Town.

Ernest F. Houfton was the village Doctor, he had a surgery in one of the Avenues.

Percy Bond Houfton was the architect of the Institute and the Drill Hall.

John Plowright Houfton, brother of Arthur, and Ernest was possibly the most well known, for as general manager of the Bolsover Colliery Company, he was instrumental in establishing the Mansfield Colliery and the village.

John P. Houfton had a distinguished career and added many additional accomplishments to his name including being made Mayor of Mansfield in 1912. In 1914 he was presented to the King and Queen in Mansfield, and a greater acclamation came in June 1929 when he was knighted and became Sir John Plowright Houfton.[23]

The people of Forest Town would no doubt have shared in the joy of these events, knowing that Sir John and his family had helped their community to develop and grow. Together, whatever their status, they were all families that belonged to the foundation years of Forest Town.

NOTES

1 Mansfield & North Notts Advertiser 1 November 1907.
2 Copy of Programme in Private Hands.
3 As above.
4 School Logbooks in private hands.
5 Mansfield & North Notts Advertiser 22 July 1910.
6 Mothers Union Minute Book in private hands.
7 Mansfield & North Notts Advertiser 30 March 1906.
8 Mansfield & North Notts Advertiser 12 June 1908.
9 Mansfield Chronicle 11 September 1908.
10 Mansfield & North Notts Advertiser 5 March 1909.
11 Mansfield Reporter & Sutton Times 20 November 1914.
12 Mansfield Chronicle 29 June 1916.
13 Mansfield & North Notts Advertiser 5 October 1906.
14 Mansfield & North Notts Advertiser 7 February 1908.
15 Mansfield & North Notts Advertiser 1 January 1909.
16 Mansfield & North Notts Advertiser 21 September 1906.
17 Mansfield & North Notts Advertiser 29 May 1908.
18 Mansfield Reporter and Sutton Times 27 November 1914.
19 Mansfield Chronicle 12 August 1915.
20 Commonwealth War Graves www.cwgc.org.uk.
21 Mansfield Chronicle 12 December 1918.
24 Newspaper cuttings and photos in private hands.
25 Mansfield Reporter 7 June 1929.

20 - THE EXPANDING VILLAGE

The building of Forest Town cannot be credited to one person or one establishment. Both time and a wide variety of people have influenced it.[1] In 1900, the time and circumstances were right for sinking the Mansfield Colliery and the building of its associated village of Forest Town. Once the first sod had been turned the local environment was destined to be reshaped and a new community born.

Forest Town was built in rural surroundings. It was distant from the town and other villages, but it was within easy reach of the Colliery for which it was erected, and the miners were close to their work. When the Bolsover Colliery Company established the new village, they considered the needs of the workforce and their families. With the essential amenities of shops, school, church and buildings such as the Institute and the Drill Hall the community had a firm foundation on which it could develop and expand.

As production at the Mansfield (Crown Farm) Colliery increased so did the working population and the need for more houses grew. Shops and houses had been built on the main Clipstone Road, and a new street, named George Street, was built off of this with a few terraced houses. George Street stopped short at the fields which ran at the back of all the shops on Clipstone Road. Shire horses from Travellers Rest Farm were a regular sight in the fields.

House and shops on Clipstone Road, with George Street in the centre of the picture, seen from the grounds of the Drill Hall

In 1910 C. Hepton, (Joiner & Undertaker), and W. Bingham, (Carter) were known to live there.[2] By 1915 the occupants were

№ 1 *Wm Hammond* — № 2 *Wm Bingham*
№ 3 *John Piggford* — № 4 *Chris Rothwell*
№ 5 *Albert Flower* — № 6 *Reuben Tebbett*
№ 7 *Jos Mallender* — № 8 *Job Perkins*
№ 9 *Chris Hepton* — №10 *William Richardson*

The land tax records list them all as houses with the exception of № 9 which was a house, stable and workshop.[3]

By 1915 detached houses were gradually being erected on the road leading out of the village towards Clipstone [Kings Clipstone]. It was still called Clipstone Road, and the names of the occupants were listed in Linney's Almanac;

W. Harper	Contractor	*C. Hilton*	Contractor
G. Murkin	Contractor	*J. T. Taylor*	Contractor
A. Scott	Contractor	*A. Faulkner*	Contractor
J. Wood	Gamekeeper	*W. Ashford*	Gardener
Mr Kirkham	Coal Dealer		

No indication is given of where on Clipstone Road the houses were, some may have been on the side roads which eventually became known as Lime Grove and Poplar Grove. They were properties which had ample land, with room for fruit trees and livestock such as hens, pigs, and possibly horses.

Forest Town was expanding in all directions. In 1911 plans were passed for eight cottages to be erected in Old Mill Lane for the Mansfield Woodhouse Smallholding Society, these were named the Smallholdings.[4] Each smallholding had approximately 5 acres of land, a good sized family house built in the same style with outbuildings such as pigsties and loose boxes.[5] The first people to live in the Smallholdings were the families of;

James Gibson	*John James Cantrill*
John Morris	*Albert King*
John Porter	*George Edward Booth*
John Green	*George Allsop* [6]

Old Mill Lane sometimes known as Woodhouse Lane, showing two of the Smallholdings

As with most colliery villages there were houses for managers, the people who were looked up to. These houses were known as 'The Villas' and built on Eakring Road, and from there both the colliery and the village could be overlooked. In 1914 the villa where Mr Bingley, the colliery manager lived (later Mr Carter) was described as being situated in over one acre of land. It had;

A dining room, drawing room, hall & conservatory,
Sitting room, kitchen and scullery/pantry.
Four bedrooms, bathroom, W.C., landings and attics.
Outside was a greenhouse, washhouse, nice garden, lawn
and it had an asphalt road to the house.[7]

What date the 'Villas' were built is unknown, but it would have been in the early days of the village development.

Throughout the years services to improve the quality of village life took place. In January 1908 the newspapers reported that Mansfield Council had agreed to erect a number of street lamps on Main Avenue.[8] A few months later a further decision was made to erect street lamps between Forest Town and Sherwood Hall.[9]

Consideration had also being given to the state of the roads and the safety of pedestrians. In March 1908 it was recommended that a kerbed and channelled footpath be laid 5ft [1524mm] in width on the North West side of Clipstone Road from the Travellers Rest to the junction with Old Mill Lane.[10]

In September 1909 it was reported at the monthly meeting of the Mansfield District Council that the Forest Town sewage scheme was now complete.[11]

From those early days when the start of both the colliery and village began, Forest Town has continued to expand. Industry, events, and people, have influenced the village to give it the character it has today. It has developed over time, and has withstood the years of war, strikes, and the loss of its foundation industry, coal mining. New industry has now taken over and brought with it new people. The landscape has continued to change and yet the initial character of the early village remains.

Each aspect of this village history can be expanded for there is still much to be discovered, both about the people, and their activities. Everyone and everything is individual in their content, and yet as a whole they are part of a fascinating local history. Within these pages, the foundations of Forest Town's history have been laid, a history that will continue to grow and evolve with the passing of time.

NOTES

1. Author's Dissertation, Advanced Certificate in Local History, June 1994.
2. Linneys Almanac 1910.
3. Land Tax PRO IR 58/5534343.
4. Mansfield & North Notts Advertiser 10 November 1911.
5. Land Tax PRO Ref IR 58 55377.
6. School Admission Registers in private hands.
7. Land Tax PRO Ref IR 58 55377.
8. Mansfield & North Notts Advertiser 10 January 1908.
9. Mansfield & North Notts Advertiser 15 May 1908.
10. Mansfield & North Notts Advertiser 6 March 1908.
11. Notts Free Press 10 Sept 1909.

The expanding village.

A postcard circa 1916, that many soldiers stationed at Clipstone Camp would have sent home to family and friends.

Forest Town was the nearest village to the camp.

BIBLIOGRAPHY

Anderson M. *H J Wilson, Fighter For Freedom (*1953).
Brisco J. P. *Nottingham & Derbyshire at the Opening of the 20th Century.*
Gibson Walter *The Concealed Coalfield HMSO (1913).*
Griffin A. R *Mining In The East Midlands 1550 - 1947* (1971).
Griffin A. R *The Nottinghamshire Coalfield 1881-1981* (Ashbourne 1981).
Haigh Bernard *A Centenary History 1889 -1989* (1989).
Harrod W. *The History of Mansfield and its Environs (*Mansfield 1986*)*
Jones L. *The Modern Building Record Vol 3 (*1912).
Share Joseph *Firelight Flashes* (Chicago Ill. 1937).
Walcot Gibson D.sc *The Concealed Coalfield* (1913)
Waller R. J. *The Dukeries Transformed* (Oxford 1983).
Williams J. E. *The Derbyshire Miners* (1962).

Unpublished Work.

Marples P. Dissertation, Advanced Certificate in Local History, University of Nottingham, June 1994, *Forest Town, The Foundation and Development of a Twentieth Century Coal Mining Village in Nottinghamshire.*

Marples P. Dissertation, MA in Local & Regional History, University of Nottingham, September 1997, *Mansfield and the Impact of the Great War.*

Newspapers.

Derbyshire Times.
Mansfield Chronicle Advertiser.
Mansfield & North Notts Advertiser.
Mansfield Reporter.

Newspaper Cutting Collection.

Midland Gazette
Nottingham Express.
Nottingham Guardian.
Rushcliffe Advertiser.
Sutton Free Press.
Sheffield Telegraph.
The Courier (Chesterfield).
Yorkshire Herald.

Directories

Kellys 1900 - 1920.
Linney's Almanac 1908 - 1920.

Pamphlets & Periodicals.

Bolsover Colliery Quarterly News.
Bolsover Jubilee Souvenir 1889-1939.
Clipstone Sale Catalogue 10th May 1945
Welbeck Newsletter Issue № 8 Winter 1998

GENERAL INDEX

98th Brigade, 118

Accident, 24, 61, 131
Admission Registers, 58, 103
Aircraft, 86
Airman, 86
Allotment/s, 75, 126, 127
Ambulance, 122
Ambulance Brigade, 107
Ambulance Division, 129
Ancaster stone, 40
Ancaster Stone Font, 42
Anglican Church, 33, 37, 39, 46
Annual dinner, 83
Annual Exhibition, 126
Archbishop of York, 106
Archdeacon, 43, 99
Architect/s, 19, 27, 39, 40, 42, 48, 76, 77, 90, 132
Army, 111, 113, 116
Assistant Under Manager, 51
Assurance Agent, 47
Assurance Superintendent, 47
Attorney General, 90, 98

Bandmaster, 40, 82, 93
Baptism Register/s, 45, 50, 55
Baptism Registers, 120
Baptisms, 43, 45, 50, 55
Barber, 71, 72
Barn, 48
Barnsley bed, 9
Bazaar/s, 35, 37, 42, 43, 95, 98, 99, 128
BCC, 75
Beer House Keeper, 15
Beer Off, 72
Bible Class, 36, 129
Bicycle, 61
Billiard rooms, 78
Billiards, 89, 93
Bishop, 39, 43, 99
Blacksmith, 51
Bolsover Collieries, 108
Bolsover Colliery, 7, 19, 20, 21, 27, 53, 103, 108, 122
Bolsover Colliery Company, 2, 7, 9, 11, 12, 19, 20, 21, 23, 24, 27, 28, 30, 36, 40, 67, 68, 75, 77, 78, 79, 87, 89, 90, 92, 98, 105, 107, 111, 113, 125, 127, 132, 135
Bolsover Colliery Company Ltd/ Limited, 19, 76
Bolsover Colliery Company's agents, 11
Bolsover Company, 19, 24, 25
Bolsover Company's, 9, 75
Boot & Shoe Dealer, 71
Boots, 67
Borough Band, 49
Bowling, 84
Bowling Clubs, 83
Bowling Green, 78,, 87 118
Boxer, 100
Boy Scouts, 129
Boys' Brigade, 40, 85, 86, 89, 90, 92, 93, 98, 107, 108, 111, 119, 121, 122, 125, 129
Brass Band, 49, 81, 85, 97, 127
Brewers, 21, 47
Brewery, 47
Brewster Sessions, 21
Bridge/s, 19, 21
British Legion, 122
Bronchitis, 119
Broseley tiles, 40
Bugle Band, 86, 92, 122
Builder/s, 19, 20, 27, 39, 77
Building fund, 43, 49, 54
Bulwell stone, 40
Burial ground, 43, 50
Burial/s, 43, 45, 50
Butcher, 67, 68, 70, 71, 72
Byron Quartet, 97

Cadet Corps, 40, 92, 107
Cadets, 86, 93, 111, 121, 125
Canary whitewood, 40
Canon Prior, 35
Caretaker, 56, 62, 78, 81, 93
Carpenter, 131
Carpenters Arms, 70
Carter, 71, 72, 135
Catholic Church, 3
Census, 14, 15, 61, 97
Century Opera Company, 100
Certificated, 61
Certificated Assistant, 58
Certificated Master, 58
Chapel, 47, 49, 50, 52, 53, 54, 95, 117, 128
Chapel school, 49
Chapel/school room, 48
Chaplain, 92, 131
Chesterfield Estate Company, 28
Chickenpox, 61
Choir, 33, 40, 120, 122, 129
Choral Society, 129
Chorister, 119
Christian Endeavour, 129
Christmas, 111, 130
Church, 33, 35, 36, 37, 39, 40, 42, 43, 44, 45, 46, 50, 57, 98, 117, 118, 119, 122, 129, 131, 135
Church Army, 33
Church Building Fund, 37
Church Extension Society, 35
Church Hall, 37
Church of England, 104
Church Officers, 42
Churchwardens, 43
Churchyard, 45, 120, 122
Cinder track, 78
Clergy, 40, 42
Clerk of works, 39
Clipstone Camp, 55, 85, 86, 114, 115, 116, 117, 119, 120
Club, 25, 75, 79, 91, 125, 130
Coal, 2, 7, 9, 11, 21, 23, 24, 25, 26, 27, 29, 35, 42, 49, 75, 79, 97, 100, 112, 125
Coal carts, 57
Coal Dealer, 136
Coal dust, 75
Collieries, 21
Colliery, 2, 9, 11, 12, 13, 14, 16, 19, 20, 21, 22, 23, 24, 25, 26, 27, 28, 29, 30, 46, 57, 75, 78, 79, 82, 83, 90, 97, 98, 99, 100, 103, 104, 108, 113, 122, 125, 135, 137
Colliery Band, 46, 75, 82, 86, 90, 95, 112, 113, 121, 125
Colliery Company, 11, 27, 28, 109, 113
Colliery Cottages, 14, 19
Colliery manager, 12
Colliery officials, 108
Colliery Prize Band, 129
Colliery village, 14
Columbia Record Company, 101
Committee, 81, 95, 104
Committee Book, 54
Committee members, 81
Committee room, 78
Commonwealth war grave, 119
Concert hall, 78, 83
Concerts, 37, 55, 79, 83, 93, 95, 98, 117, 128
Confectioner, 72
Constables, 86, 121
Contractor, 136
Conveyance, 47
Co-op, 55, 67, 68, 69, 72
Co-operative Society, 67
Co-operative Store, 70
Coronation, 60, 61, 103, 104
Cottagers, 126
Cottages, 19, 27, 105, 136

Council School/s, 37, 58, 64
County Council, 57
Cricket, 78, 79, 81, 82, 83, 85, 86, 93, 108, 118, 129
Cricket Club, 81, 84, 86, 89
Cricket Ground, 77, 126
Cricket pavilion, 78
Cricket pitch, 78
Crown Farm, 9, 13, 14, 17, 19, 20, 21, 57, 58, 116, 125
Crown Farm Colliery, 9, 13, 130, 131
Crown Farm Pit, 2
Crownie, 2, 9, 13, 125
Curate, 35, 37, 40, 99, 131
Cycle races, 79
Cycle Stores, 71
Cycle track, 79, 81
Cyclist/s, 79, 86

Dance, 37
Day man, 131
DCM, 95, 122
Death, 111, 116, 119, 120, 131
Derbyshire Record Office, 19, 125
Died, 14, 15, 62, 101, 103, 130, 131
Director of Education, 58
Directory, 71
Doctor, 130, 132
Drapery, 67, 68, 128
Drill Hall, 40, 42, 53, 55, 89, 90, 91, 92, 93, 94, 95, 96, 98, 101, 105, 111, 112, 113, 121, 122, 132, 135
Druggist, 72
Duchess of Portland, 106
Duke, 9, 36, 108
Duke of Portland, 2, 6, 9, 11, 12, 13, 15, 20, 33, 39, 40, 47, 53, 57, 84, 89, 96, 108, 106, 112
Duke of Portland's agent/s, 12, 20, 39, 90
Duke's land agent, 11

Ecclesiastical commissioners, 39
Education Committee, 57
Education minutes, 62
Empire Battalion, 117
Empire Day, 60, 103
Engine Winder, 51
Enginewright, 25
Epidemics, 61
Exemption certificate, 60
Farm/s, 5, 6, 7, 11, 12, 13, 14, 16, 57, 58, 103
Farmers, 11, 13, 16, 55
Feast holiday, 60
Fire Brigade, 129
First World War, 55, 85
Fish & Chips, 71
Fish Shop, 71, 72
Football club, 35
Football field, 108
Footwear, 70
Forest Town Chapel, 50
Forest Town Co-op, 68
Forest Town Miners' Institute, 81
Forest Town School, 125
Forest Town Stores, 21, 71, 72
Forest Town String Band, 126
Foundation stones, 48
Friendly Societies, 125
Funeral, 61

Gamekeeper, 136
Gardener, 136
General Dealer, 71, 72
General manager, 12, 24, 25, 27, 53, 67, 68, 79, 90, 132
Girls' Brigade, 93, 128
Glee Club, 40, 95
Globe Tea Company, 71
Grammar School, 60
Great War, 111, 123
Greengrocer, 71
Greenhouses, 78
Grocer, 71
Grocery, 67, 68, 70
Gymnasium, 93
Gymnastic, 89

Halifax Place Mission, Nottingham, 53
Harvest festivals, 55
Head Teacher, 58, 61, 62
Headmaster, 58, 59, 61
Headmistress, 60
Horse and cart, 67, 69
Horticultural Exhibition, 127
Horticultural Society, 70, 126
Hospital, 101, 129, 130

Illness, 61
Incumbent, 43
Indenture, 47
Infant room, 59
Infant School logbook, 64
Infants Department, 60, 62
Influenza, 61, 119
Injured, 100, 131
Inspectors, 59, 62
Institute, 3, 75,76, 77, 78, 79, 81, 83, 85, 86, 87, 89, 104, 105, 107, 108, 118, 120, 121, 130, 132, 135
Institute grounds, 105, 107

Joiner & Undertaker, 135

King, 103, 104, 105, 106, 108, 113, 133
King and country, 95, 111, 112, 131
King John's Palace, 5
Kings Athletic Stores, 21
Kingsway Hall, 92, 101
Knighted, 133
KOYLI, 84, 119

Labourer, 47
Lamps, 59
Land tax, 135
Land Tax Records, 64
Land Tax Survey, 28
Langwith Lodge, 39
Lessons, 59, 60, 63, 99
Library, 78, 79
Licensed Victualler, 15
Linney's Almanac, 70, 71, 136
Linneys Directories, 82
Local Government Board, 57
Lockwood, 131
Logbook/s, 59, 60, 61, 64

Manager, 68, 78, 90, 122, 130, 137
Mansfield (Crown Farm) Colliery, 75, 98, 112, 135
Mansfield Circuit, 53
Mansfield Colliery, 2, 9, 11, 12, 13, 14, 16, 17, 19, 22, 23, 26, 27, 48, 75, 79, 81, 82, 84, 85, 86, 90, 92, 93, 95, 97, 98, 99, 101, 103, 106, 108, 111, 113, 114, 116, 118, 119, 122, 125, 126, 127, 128, 129, 131, 135
Mansfield Colliery Band, 81, 83, 90, 98
Mansfield Colliery Bugle Band, 129
Mansfield Colliery Company, 13, 19
Mansfield Colliery Company Limited, 19
Mansfield Colliery Cricket Team, 130
Mansfield Colliery Institute, 79, 131, 132
Mansfield Colliery Orchestral Band, 129

Mansfield Colliery Silver Prize Band, 129
Mansfield Co-operative Society, 67
Mansfield Council, 19, 137
Mansfield District Council, 137
Mansfield Military Band, 129
Mansfield Railway, 112, 107, 111, 118
Mansfield Road, 14
Mansfield Town Council, 19
Mansfield Woodhouse Council, 19, 20, 21, 22
Mansfield Woodhouse Council School, 38
Mansfield Woodhouse District Council, 27
Mansfield Woodhouse Hospital, 21
Mansfield Woodhouse Parish Church, 33, 36
Marriages, 46, 50, 120, 131
Married, 61, 98, 99, 120, 132
Mayor, 128, 133
Measles, 61
Medals, 84, 104, 109, 122, 125
Methodist, 47, 48, 53, 70, 86, 89, 117, 120
Methodist Chapel, 49
Methodist Conference, 50
Methodist schoolroom, 57
Methodists, 53, 55
Metropolitan Opera Company, 100
Midland Railway, 21
Military, 85, 96, 111, 112, 114, 116, 119, 122
Military funeral, 120
Military sports, 118
Milliner, 71, 72
Miner, 9, 27, 28, 29, 30, 47,, 51, 57, 75, 85, 90 97, 98, 99, 100, 101, 105, 106, 111, 112, 113
Miners Institute, 75, 77, 80, 132
Miners Welfare Building, 87
Minute Books, 67
Mission Church, 33, 34, 36, 37, 45, 46, 127
Mission Sunday School, 36
Mixed and Infants Depts, 58
Mixed Dept./Department 58, 59, 60
Mixed Division, 59
Morning chapel, 40, 42
Mothers Sewing Meeting, 42
Mothers Union, 128
Mount Durran, 127
Musical entertainment, 49, 85, 90, 98

National celebrations, 60
National Defence, 90, 98
National events, 61
National Friendly Society, 125
Neuralgia, 61
New Sherwood School, 64
New Sherwood Council School, 57
Newgate Lane schools, 57
Newlands Farm, 5, 6, 21
Newsagent, 71, 72
Night soil men, 29, 30
Non-conformist, 104
North aisle, 40, 42
Nottinghamshire Archives, 76, 77
Notts League, 84
Notts. and Derbyshire Regiment, 122
Nurse, 62, 119

Off-licence, 21
Oil lamps, 28
Old Comrades Association, 129
Omnibus, 71, 118
Omnibus Proprietor, 71, 72
Open-air service, 49
Orchestral Band, 37
Organ, 33, 40, 46, 121
Organist, 33, 131
Osslington Hall, 126

Parish Church, 36, 50, 99
Parish Hall, 129
Parish Rooms, 37
Parsonage, 36, 39
Patronal Festival, 129
Peace celebrations, 121
Peace Memento card., 86
Peace Parade, 87
Peace Thanksgiving, 86
Petrol pump, 73
Plaque, 69, 119
Pneumonia, 119
Police, 129
Policeman, 30
Post box, 73
Post Office, 70, 71, 72, 73
Postmaster, 70
Primitive, 57, 104, 105
Primitive Methodism, 49
Primitive Methodist, 47, 128
Primitive Methodist Chapel, 47, 50, 51, 52, 53, 54, 55, 89
Primitive Methodist schoolroom, 126
Primitive Methodists, 49, 53, 121, 129
Prince Charles [Public House], 21, 69, 72
Principle assistant, 58
Printer, 47
Prize Band, 82, 86
Provision Dealer, 70
Public Elementary School, 64
Public House, 21
Pulpit, 40

Queen, 83, 98, 103, 104, 105, 106, 108, 113, 133
Queens Coll., 118
Queens Hall, 99
Queens Own Yorkshire Dragoon/s, 79, 126
Queens Regiment, 121

Railway Branch Line, 20
Railway Porter, 51
Railways, 11
RAMC, 117, 122
RE, 122
Reading room, 78, 79
Rector, 131
Red Cross, 118
Registers, 33, 43, 45, 62, 120
Religious instruction, 59
River Maun, 6, 7
Roll of Honour, 120, 121
Roxsall, 118
Royal, 86, 107
Royal Air Force, 86
Royal Engineers, 117
Royal Fusiliers, 118
Royal Horse Artillery, 114
Royalty, 103
Russian Hut, 96

Sailors, 86, 112, 121, 122
Sales of work, 35, 55
Sanitary Inspector, 20
Scavenging, 20, 27
Scholars, 52
School, 7, 29, 47, 51, 57, 58, 59, 60, 61, 62, 63, 64, 68, 97, 103, 105, 117, 120, 127, 128, 129, 135
School Admission Registers, 125
School chapel, 47
School curriculum, 59
School holidays, 60
School inspectors, 60
School lessons, 64

School logbook, 58, 59, 62, 103
School nurse, 62
School work book, 63
Schoolroom, 49
Senior school, 60
Sewage, 11, 20, 137
Sewing classes, 35, 128
Sherwood Colliery, 21, 24
Sherwood Foresters, 84, 112, 114
Sherwood Hall, 6, 7, 13, 15, 91, 103, 114, 116, 126, 127, 137
Shoemaker, 71, 72
Shop/s, 1, 2, 5, 67, 68, 69, 70, 71, 72, 73, 118, 135
Shopkeepers, 55, 67, 70, 71
Shrove Tuesday, 60
Silver Band, 122
Silver Prize Band, 40, 82, 129
Singing Miner, 97
Sinker, 25
Sinking, 2, 9, 12, 16, 19, 22, 23, 24, 25, 27, 75, 98, 135
Smallholding Society, 136
Smoke room, 78
Soldier, 51, 55, 61, 85, 86, 111, 112, 113, 114, 115, 116, 117, 118, 119, 120, 121, 122
South Nottinghamshire Yeomanry, 14
Southwell Branch Line, 21
Spiky Island, 28
Sports ground, 86, 118
St Alban's, 33, 40, 42, 43, 45, 46, 50, 86, 95, 99, 105, 118, 120, 121, 122, 129, 131, 132
St Alban's Church, 39, 119
St Alban's churchyard, 22, 120, 122
St David's, 37
St David's Mission, 33, 34, 35, 127
St Edmund's, 33, 50
St John's, 97
St John's Ambulance Brigade, 40, 125
St Lawrence, 98
St Lawrence's, 35, 57, 98
St Nicholas', 93
St Patrick's Catholic, 54
St Peter's, 35, 98
Stables, 13, 15, 69
Staff, 59, 60, 61, 120
Star Cards, 51
Star Registers, 51
Stone laying ceremony, 39, 42, 48, 49, 95
Stone Laying Ceremony, 41
Stores, 71
Straight Mile, 6
Street lamps, 137
Sunday School, 36, 51, 120
Sunday School Anniversaries, 51
Sunday School Reports, 51
Sunday School treat, 52
Sunday Schools, 122
Superintendent preacher, 47
Surgeon, 92
Surgery, 132

Tailor- made, 70
Taxi, 70, 73, 118, 119
Taylors Stores, 72
Teachers, 58, 59, 60, 61, 62, 64, 120, 128
Telephone, 73
Temporary buildings, 64
Temporary iron building, 57, 59
Temporary schools, 57
Tennis Club, 79
Tennis courts, 78, 80, 118
Territorial Army, 92
Territorial Force, 113
The Avenues, *See Aven*ues
The Duke of Portland, 41
Tin bath, 29
Tin chapel, 54, 56
Toilet, 28, 29
Top Hard, 9, 25
Track, 80
Travellers Rest, 6, 7, 13, 14, 15, 16, 17, 19, 39, 47, 48, 58, 89, 137
Travellers Rest Farm, 53, 135
Travellers Rest Inn, 15
Trustees, 47, 48
Tug-of-war team, 81

Uncertificated, 61
Uncertificated Mistress, 58
Uncertificated teacher, 61
Undermanager, 90, 99
UPS [University & Public Schools] Brigade, 118
Urban District Council, 122

Vestries, 48
Vicar, 33, 35, 36, 39, 40, 129
Victoria Hall, 98
Villas, 137

WAACs, 120
Wakefield, 30, 42, 48
Walkers Plantation, 6, 116, 117
War, 49, 52, 70, 71, 81, 83, 85, 86, 111, 112, 114, 115, 117, 118, 119, 120, 122, 131, 137
War Memorial, 122
Warsop church, 99
Water supply, 19, 20, 27
Wedding, 131, 132
Welbeck Abbey, 9, 112
Welbeck Estate/s, 5, 6, 9
Weldon stone, 40
Welkin Ring, 104
Wesleyan, 53, 55
Wesleyan building, 55
Wesleyan Chapel, 53, 54
Wesleyan Methodist, 86
Wesleyan Methodist Chapel, 53
Wesleyan Methodists, 54, 95, 104, 105, 121
Wesleyan register, 55
Whist, 84
Whist Drive, 37
White feathers, 112
Whitsuntide, 60
Whooping cough, 61
Workman's Institute, 77
Workmens Club, 77

Yarmouth, 93
Yeomanry, 14
York Street Council School, 64

PLACE NAME INDEX

Alfreton, 116
Algona, 50
America, 50, 99, 101
Avenues, 2, 19, 20, 27, 28, 30, 31, 32, 55, 82, 105, 106, 116, 125, 132
  Main Avenue, 28, 68, 69, 72, 137
  First Avenue, 28, 53, 58, 63, 89, 105, 111, 114, 127
  Second Ave/Avenue, 28, 53, 54, 55, 58, 63, 68, 89, 105, 106, 107, 125
  Third Avenue, 28, 54, 55, 114
  Fourth Avenue, 32, 55, 58, 113, 114
  Fifth Ave/Avenue, 28, 54, 55, 58, 75, 78, 113, 114. 125
  Sixth Avenue, 54, 58, 113, 114, 130
  Seventh Avenue, 55, 114
  Eighth Ave/Avenue, 28, 55, 58, 114, 119, 125
  Ninth Ave/Avenue, 54, 67, 114, 125

Beardall Street, 97
Belfast, 79
Belgium, 112
Berry Hill, 15, 126
Berry Hill Road, 15
Big Barn Lane, 129
Blackwell, 116
Bolsover, 7, 9, 23, 27, 77, 90, 107, 116
Boulogne, 119
Bridlington, 93
Brighton, 27
Britain, 111, 112
British Columbia, 106
Buckinghamshire, 101
Burton-on-Trent, 82

Cambridge, 118
Carter Lane, 98, 129
Cheshire, 118
Chesterfield, 12, 19, 27, 30, 76, 77
Church Street, 70
Clipstone, 5, 6, 9, 15, 20, 131, 136
Clipstone Drive, 6
Clipstone Road, 21, 28, 33, 53, 54, 62, 67, 68, 69, 70, 71, 72, 78, 87, 89, 104, 105, 117, 135, 136, 137
Colwyn, 27, 82
Colwyn Bay, 27
Covent Garden, 100
Creswell, 9, 23, 30, 77, 90, 107, 125

Derbyshire, 1, 2, 9, 12, 23, 75, 104, 112, 125
Dinnington, 27
Dulwich, 118

Eakring Road, 13, 137
Eastwood, 12
Elmhurst Road, 1
England, 100, 101, 106, 113

Forest Town, 1, 2, 5, 6, 9, 20, 26, 27, 28, 30, 32, 33, 35, 36, 37, 39, 40, 42, 43, 46, 47, 48, 49, 50, 52, 53, 55, 56, 57, 59, 63, 64, 67, 68, 70, 71, 72, 73, 75, 76, 77, 78, 79, 82, 83, 84, 85, 86, 87, 89, 90, 96, 97, 98, 99, 101, 103, 104, 105, 107, 108, 111, 112, 113, 114, 115, 116, 117, 118, 119, 120, 121, 122, 123, 125, 126, 127, 128, 129, 130, 131, 132, 133, 135, 136, 137
Forest Town Crossroads, 6, 33
France, 78, 119, 120

George Street, 54, 135
Germany, 112
Glasgow, 59
Golders Green, 118
Grimethorpe, 82
Guernsey, 127

Hamps, 118
High Street, 68, 70, 71
Hucknall, 30, 81, 82, 97, 98, 125, 130
Hucknall Torkard, 97
Huddersfield, 131

Iowa, 50

Kings Clipstone, 5, 6, 136
Kirkby Woodhouse, 125

Leeds, 12
Leeming Street, 21
Leicester, 81
Leicestershire, 125
Lime Grove, 136
Lincoln, 82
London, 27, 39, 99, 100, 101, 118
Loughton, 27
Lyndhurst, 15

Manchester, 7, 57, 117
Mansfield, 1, 5, 6, 7, 9, 15, 20, 21, 22, 23, 24, 30, 33, 35, 40, 47, 49, 57, 58, 70, 75, 78, 89, 90, 98, 100, 105, 112, 113, 114, 116, 118, 122, 127, 128, 129, 130, 131, 133
Mansfield Woodhouse, 6, 19, 20, 21, 22, 27, 33, 35, 36, 39, 40, 43, 45, 46, 47, 48, 49, 50, 57, 60, 64, 67, 122, 136
Middlesex/Middx., 118

Nanamimo, 106
New York, 50, 100
Newark, 21, 47, 113
Newell, 50
Nottingham, 53
Nottinghamshire, 1, 7, 9, 12, 35, 97, 98, 100, 103, 104, 112, 113, 125, 126
Notts, 79, 104

Old Mill Lane, 6, 33, 136, 137
Ollerton, 5, 14
Oxford, 118

Penrith, Cumberland, 27
Poplar Grove, 136

Rainworth, 6

Sheep Wash Lane, 6
Sheffield, 7
Shirebrook, 125
Sioux City, 50
Skegness, 79, 93, 132
Smallholdings, 136
Southwell, 6, 21, 39, 43, 99
St Margaret Street, 98
Staffordshire, 12, 97, 125
Stockwell Gate, 127
Stoke Poges, 101
Surrey, 118
Sussex, 118
Sutton, 45, 116
Swanwick, 82

Tipton, 97

U.S.A, 50

Warsop, 99, 129
Warsop Vale, 63, 99
Wednesbury, 97
Westminster, 39, 104
Whitwell, 30, 81, 125
Woodhouse Lane, 136
Woodhouse Road, 6
Woodville, 82
Worksop, 9, 108

Yorkshire, 12, 27, 104, 119, 125

NAME INDEX

Adams, W.J. 71
Agnini, Armando F 99
Aichman, Pte 117
Albon, Henry Alonzo 45
Albon, J. 126
Alexandra, O. 84
Allsop, George 136
Ambler, Hilda 93
 Louis 39, 40, 42
Annable, A 42
 Ethel 58
 F. 42
 Fred 131
 Frederick 58
 G. 84
 J. 81, 126
 K. 82
 Miss 128
 Mrs 42, 128
 S. 128
 T. 126
Archbishop of York, 106
Arnold, C.P. 118
 F. 71, 72
Arrowsmith, Vera 45
Ashford, W. 136
Audisio, Pietro 99
Ayres, Sydney 45

Bacon, Sydney Herbert 131, 132
Bainbridge, (jun.) Oswald 78
 Emerson 78, 90, 98
 Emerson Muschamp 9, 90
 Gladys 93
 Mr 78, 127
 Mrs 42, 91
 O.J. 81
 Oswald 78, 87, 90
Baldwin, Henry 27
Banner, 55
 Bernard Jackson 55
 Ethel 54
 J. 126
 Mary Jane 55
 Saml 54
 Samuel 55
Bantock, Mrs 27
Barfoot, J. 42
Barker, Joe 45
 P. 42
Barlow, Councillor 19
 Willam 25
Barnes, 79
 J. 81, 84, 118
 W. 72
Barthorpe, W. 95
Beazley, 55
 C.T. 54
Beeton, Mr 62
Bell, 81J.A.
Bennet Furnishing Co, 59
Bennett, Thomas Frederick 45
Beresford, A. 42
 Albert 25
 R. 92
Betts, 70
 W. 71
 William 54
Bingham, E. 48
 F. 48
Bingham, Miss 128, 129
 N. Miss 128
 W. 126, 135
 Wm 135
Bingley, Captain 40
Bingley, J. 37, 42, 79, 81, 90, 92, 108
 Joe 127
 John 24
 Kathleen 42
 Mr 62, 78, 137
 Mrs 108
 Mrs or Miss's, 128
Bircumshaw, A. 129
 Aaron 92
Birkett, W. 42,81
Bishop of Southwell, 43, 99
Black, A. 118
Blackburn, 129
Blood, Reginald 54
Bloor, I. 42
Blount, R. 81
Blythe, see Vallance & Blythe 67
Bode, 129
Bodell, Florence 128
 Florence Allen 58
 Miss 61
Boden, 50, 128
 Frank 114
 T. 81
Bolland, Olive 45
Bonser, Mr 129
Boot, A. 84, 129
 W.E. 122
Booth, George Edward 136
Bosworth, T. 81, 84
Bowen, J. 126
Bowman Bros, 42
Bowyer, 55
Bradbury (nee) Naomi, 59
Bradshaw, G 123
Brain, A. 81
Brindley & Foster, 46
Bristowe, C.J. 58
Brown, G. 93
 John Walter 45
 Major 86
 W. 121
Bryer, J. 81
Bugg, Phyllis 93
Bull, H Rev 86, 92, 122, 129131
 H. 42
 Harry 40, 45, 128
 Margaret 35, 62, 128
 Margery 93
 Mr 62
Bull, Rev 35, 95, 104,113, 120, 121, 128
Bullock, 25, 32
 brothers 25
 G. 123
 J. 126
 May 54
Bunfield, C. 104, 108
 Mrs 108
Burton, J.E. 123
Butcher, Frank 54
 Myles 54
 Tom 54
Buxton, A. 84
 Bertha 68

Caddy, J. 95
Cadwaller, John Wilfred 45
Cantrill, John James 136
Carr, Miss 60
Carter, F. 123
 Mr 108, 122, 137
 Mrs 52
 W. 92, 104
 W. Councillor JP 129
 W.H. 84, 95, 104,108, 121, 122
Cawthorne, J.G. 68
Chadbourne, N. 123
Charles J. Vallance and Sons, 42
Cheetham, Elizabeth 67
Chester, C. 84, 118
 G. 84, 114
 J. 84
Clark, Arthur 54
Clarke, C. 114
 W.R. 27
Clatworthy, Councillor 20
Clegg, Pte 117
Clement, 55
Coates, L.J.M. 27
Collier, C. 37
Commons, H. 42
Cook, F.P. 48
 H. 126
 Miss 48
 W. 81, 129
 William 25
Cooke, Ernest 103
 W.H. 42
 W.S. 42
Cooper, R.M 114
 W. 84, 118
Cousins, Mrs 62
Cowpe, see Liptons and Cowpe 55
Cowper, Edith 36
Cross, A. 71, 72
 H. 70
 J.H. 70
Cunliffe, Captain 33
Cupit, 50, 55
 J Bandmaster 40
 J. 93, 126
 Jack 82
 John 51
 Walter 45
Cutter, R.C. 118
Cutts, 32, 50
 G 95, 114
 George 58
 J. 84
 Joseph 103
 W. 85
 William 58

Danks, see Thomas Danks & Co Ltd, 42
Davidson, W.A. 113
Davis, 81, 108, 128
 A Supt. 40
 A. 40, 42, 81, 90
 Albert 99, 122

F. 95
Frederick 51
H. 126, 129
Lena, 131
Mollie, 131
Mr 78, 108, 131
Mrs 108, 131
Nellie 131
P. 81
W. 84, 118, 129
Daxon, H.A. 83
Mr 121
Mrs 83, 121
P Miss 131
Phyllis 121
Phyllis Mary 131, 132
Day, E. 95
Reuben 15
Dent, R. 43
Dovey, Mr 69
Dunn, R. 81

Eames, H. 129
Edward the Seventh, 103
Edwards, 129
Edwyn, Bishop of Southwell, 39
Egglestone, Mr 54
Elliott, 55
Miss, 61
Elvidge, T. 84
Exley, see William Exley & Sons,

Fairfield, T. 81, 84
Faulkner, A. 136
Arthur 67
Fisher, Richard 25
Fletcher, Mr 50
Flower, Albert 135
Foster, see Brindley & Foster 46
Foster, W.H. Rev. 33
Fox, Annie 93
Doris 93
Edith 14
Eva 93
George 58
John David 58, 103
Lily 93
T. 84
Frith, F. 71
Frost, 50
Frost, Adeline 58, 128
Miss 61

Gabbitas, A. 81
Gamble, J. 95
W.T. 61
Gambles, T.W. 61
Garton, W. 123
Gibson, James 136
Sarah 93
Gill, Margery 93
Gilliott, A. 104
Gilway, 70, 71
Gilway, T. 70, 71
Ginger Lee & Co, 57
Gittings, G. 81, 84
Lily 103
Miriam 93
Miss 129
Nina 63
Goodman, Annie 54
J.T. 71, 72, 118
Gowe, Hayden Rev 131
Green Bros. and Sykes, 19, 20, 27
Green, 19, 27, 50
Archie 54
Hy 54
John 136
Greenwood, J. 57
Guiseppe De Luca, 99
Gumm, Mrs 128
Gunn, 104
Guy, Elsie 93
Guylor, J. 42
Mrs J. 104

Hallam, J. 42
Hamilton, J.W. 126
Mrs 128
Hammond, Wm 135
Hancock, J.C. M.P, 104
Hancock, J.G. 108
Mrs 108
Handley, J. 85
Harcombe E.T. Vicar 36
E.T. Rev. 40, 90
Rev. 39
Hardwick, C. 81
Hardy, Annie 45
Hardy, F. 50
Hargreaves, E. 128
Nellie 63
S. 128
W. 81, 84
Harper, W. 136
Harrison, Mr 61
Harry Bull, Rev. 35, 43, 113
Hart, J. 129
Hartley, J.C. 118
Harvey, 15, 79, 81
Alice 93
George 15
L. 49
Leonard 47
Mary, 15
Mrs 15
Rosa 27
Tom 15
Harwood, Pte 117
Haslam, Elizabeth Anne 130
Connie 93
family 130
William 130
Heald, W. 123
Heath, Mr 69
Mrs 52
Henderson, H. 90, 99
H.G.M. 97
Hepton, C 126, 135
Chris 135
Hickman, W. 84, 85
Hill, G. 83
Hilton, C. 136
Mrs 52
Hinton, J. 92
J. Lieut 40
John William 58
William 58
Hirst, A. 97
Hobson, Joyce Mavis 50
Sarah Ann 50
Hodgett, Rachel 97
Hodgetts, Hilda 93
Holdsworth, Thomas 7
Hole & Co, 21, 47
Hole see James Hole & Co Ltd, 21
Holes the Brewers, 47
Holland, Capt. 118
Mrs 42
N. 85
W. 90, 97, 99
W.T. 97
William 97, 99
Holloway, N.J. 118
Hopewell, J. 81, 126
Hopkinson, F. 97
Horan, 129
Houfton & Johnson, 19, 27

Houfton, A.F. 69
Agnes 108
Arthur Frederick 132
C. 81
Charles 12
Doctor 130
Dr 81
E.H. MD 92
Ernest F. 132
family 132
J.P. 81, 104, 108, 113
J.W. 108
John P. 27, 78, 79, 83, 90, 112, 113, 133
John Plowright 12, 24, 25, 53, 68, 122, 132, 133
Mr 53, 113
Mrs 108
Percy Bond 27, 77, 90, 132
Percy F. 76
W.O. 81
William 114
Houghton, P. 92
P.W. Lieut. 40
Hovey, Charles Howell 28
Howard, John 15
Hudson, Miss 131
Huggetts, Mrs 52
Hunt, P. Miss 118
Hurst (nee), Elizabeth see Newton, Elizabeth 14
Hursthouse, Mrs 52

Ingham, F.W. 114

J.W. Singer & Sons, 42
James Hole & Co Ltd, 21
Jennings, Mrs 128
Jepson, A. 62
Jessop, 32
G. 131
John Robinson & Co, 127
Johnson, D. 84
Jones & Willis Ltd, 42
Jones, G. 118
Mr 108
Mrs 108
R.L. 81, 108

Keeton, 55
J. 104
William 54

Kelk, J. 123
Kellet, Colonel 7
Kelshaw, W.H.H. Rev 53
Kemp, 69, 70
G. 129
Mr 69
Kempin, Alfred 55
Edna Mary 55
Harriett 55
King Edward the Seventh, 103
King Edward, 103
King George, 60, 83, 103, 104, 105
Fifth, 60, 103, 104
V, 83, 104
King, 104, 105, 106, 108, 113, 133
King, Albert 136
Kings Athletic Stores, 21
Kingston, A.W. 90, 97, 99, 129
Alfred 97, 98, 99, 100
Alfred W. 90
Alfred Webster 97
Alfred Webster (Morgan) 101
Elizabeth 97
Frederick 97
Jane 97
John 97
John T. 97
Lieut. 40
Morgan 43, 98, 99, 100, 101
W. 37, 42, 92
W.H. 90, 92, 99
W.T. 97
William 97, 98
Kirk, Mr 49
William 47
Kirkham, Mr 136
Kitchen, William 58
William Wigman 58
Kitchener, 70
Mrs 61, 71
Knowles, R.M. 104
Lacey, C.A. 92
Charles 122
F Miss 42
J Sergt. Major 40
Major 92
Lakin, T. 54
Lancashire, S. 123
Simeon 131
Landers, Mrs 42
Laycock, Michael Reverend 47
Laykin, W. 54
Lebeters, 71, 72, 73
Lee, A. 123
G. 86, 121
J. DCM & Bar 95
J. Francis 54
Mr 60, 61, 69
Robert 59
Lees, A. 81
Limb, W.G. 20
Ling, H.W. 118
Linney's, 70, 71, 136
Linneys, 82
Liptons and Cowpe, 55
Lucas, C.E. 118
Mace, Alfred 50
Charles Ambrose 50
Elizabeth Florence 50
James 113
Mallender, Jos 135
Mannion, Martin 25
Marklew, W.(A.S.) 84
Marriott, 72
Mr 71
Marsh, 55
Mattfield, Marie 99
Matzenauer, Margarete 99
Maude, Bessie 97
Mawers, 55
Meany, M. 81
Mein, W.H. 92
Mellors, Evelyn 93
Mellows, H. 84
Middleton, 55
B. 72
Midwinter, Frank 125
Millard, L. 114
Luther 51
Miller, N. 118
Millership, Albert 50
Doris 50
Nellie 50
Mills, Ed 114
Milnes, T. 84
Monks, F. 123
Moore, see T. & R. Moore, 98
Morley, Mr 131
Mrs 61, 131
Reginald Wragge 131
W. 71
Morris, E. 129
E.R. 126
John 136
Mott, E. 95
Mottishaw, Elijah 106
Sarah 106
son 106
Moult, 32
Mary 32
Nellie 32
Winnie 32
Moxon, 50
E. 114
Mrs 52
W. 123
Walter 113, 131
Munks, Second Officer 40
Munnings, Corporal 119
F. 92
F.J. 119, 123
Frederick James 131
Murden, 32, 70
Alice Annie 45
J. 81, 84
J.T. 123
John 58, 67
M Miss 42
T. 114
Thomas 58, 103
Murkin, G. 136
Murray, Mr 50
Muzio, Claudia 99

Naylor, E. 84
E.W. 84
William 114
Needham, J. 84
Phyllis Edith 45
Newcombe, C.N. 84
Newton, Edith 14
Elizabeth (nee Hurst), 14
family 17
Frank 14
Frederick John 14
George 14
James 14
Leonard 14, 58
Leonard James 103
Lucy 14
North, Ethel 60
H. 81
Oade's, G.H. 70
Oakey, H. 77
Oates, Mary Ann 45
O'Brien, J. 114
Oivers, C.O. 55
Oliver, F. 126
O'Meara, J. 95
Ordynski, Richard 99
Orridge, Sergt. 120
Osler, Eliza 70
Montague 70, 119
S. 71, 72
Shadrach 70, 73, 118
Oslers, 55, 73

Palmer, Councillor 20
Papi, Gennaro 99
Parker, 50
A. 84
Parkin, Issac 103
Parkinson, Miss 48, 128
Mr 48
Parr, Arthur 50
Edith 50
Parr, Mr 54
W. 92
Woodhall 50
Patrick, John 131
Payne, M.W. 118
Pearson, F. 84
Frank 51
Peatman, A. 123
Perkens, Job 135
Perry, George 131
Mark 58
William George 58
Peters, A.S. 95
W. 84
Philips, P.W. 81
Pickering, S.F. 123
Piggford, John 135
Place, G. 81
Pogmore, W. 43
Poole, 61, 79
Carrie Agnes 128
Miss 61
T. 84, 118
Porter, John 136
Portland, Duchess of 106
Portland, Duke of 2, 6, 9, 11, 12, 13, 15, 20, 33, 36, 39, 40, 41, 47, 53, 57, 84, 89, 90, 96, 106, 108, 112

Powell, 32
children 32
George 131
Mrs 32
Price, C. 126
Purdy, J. 84, 118
John F. 125
R. 85

Queen Mary, 83, 104, 105
Queen Victoria, 103
Queen, 79, 83, 98, 103, 104, 105, 106, 108, 133

Ramsdale, A. 71, 72
Ranby, Mrs 72
Ratcliffe ,John T. 125
Rawlins, Mrs 67
Raybould, J.H. 118
Redfern, J. 128
Miss 128
Redram, G. 50
Reggin, Alec 54
Reschiglian, Vincenzo 99
Rice, 84J.
Richardson, Archdeacon 43, 99
E. 114, 123
Ernest 131
William 135
Richmond, W. 81
Riley, H. 129
Roberts, Ann 128
Robinson, Mr 22, 62
Mrs 128
W. 48, 49
William 47
Robottom, C.A. 114
Robson, William Sir M.P. 90, 98
Roe, H........ 51
Mr 130
Roper, Albert 51
Rose, W. 42
Rothier, Leon 99
Rothwell, Chris 135
Mrs 60
Naomi 59
Roulston, Harry (Henry) 82
Roulston, Harry 83, 86
Rouse, Mrs 48
Rowland, A. 97
Rowley, S. 50
Rudge, Kate 128
Kate Evelyn 58
Mary 93
Mr 58, 59, 60, 61
Mrs 42, 61
William Warren 58
Wm 58
Rutland, Arthur 47

S____, T. 118
Sales, J. 81
Sanderson, W. 126
Sarll, Doris Barbara 128
Major 113
Miss 61
Saunderson, Elizabeth 128
Saville, A.C. 118
Saxton, A. 84, 118
Sayles, Miss 128
Mrs 128
Scott, A. 136
Mr 69
Mrs 128
Sefton, J. 84
Senior, Dorothy 50
Ellen Louise 50
J Lieut. 40
J. E. 92
James Edward 50
Setti, Giulo 99
Severn, J Third Officer 40
Severn, J. 81
J.A. 92
Share, 19, 32
family 50
J. 51
Joseph 47, 50
Mr 50
Mrs 42, 50,128
Rev 50
T. 84
T.W. 81
Shaw, A. 86, 121
Sheldon, W. 123
Shelton, Charles Edward 25
Shooter, Elizabeth 60, 128
Lizzie 126
Miss 61
Shore, T.W. 79
Siedle, Edward 99
Silcock, 32
R. 84
Robert 67
Sarah 67
Simms, Councillor 19
Simpson-Alcock, J. 53

Singer, see J.W. Singer & Sons, 42
Singleton, Councillor - Mayor 128
Skey, C.H. 118
Slack, Josiah 47
Mrs 128
Sleigh, G.H. 68
Smart, F. 92
Smith, A.W 49
Albert William 47
G. 42, 84, 129
Issac and family 48
Joseph 51
Mr 61
Mrs 49, 128
Violet 54
W. 84, 118
Spencer, L. 104, 108
Mrs 108
Spooner, Clare E. 27
Clare Elizabeth 28
Stafford, Mabel Silverton 60, 128
Stafford, Miss 60, 61, 62
Stainer, Rev. 99
Stanley, 129
Edgington 125
Staton, Frank 54
J.A. 92
Stennett, 55
Stewart, Mr 48
Stone, Clara 93
Straw, Mary 93
Stubbing, T. 126
Sutton, Ethel 45
Swaby, 32, 40
C. 128
C.W. 42
First Officer 40
Septimus 67
Swain, 32
Arthur 58, 103
Miss 61
Thomas 58
Sweeny Todd, 71
Swift, T.G. 118
Sykes, see Green Bros. and Sykes
Sykes, A.C. 27
Mr 67

T. & R. Moore, 98
Tatlow, T.N. 81
Taylor, 55
F. 129
I. 123
J. 129
J.T. 136
L.B. 95
Miss 129
Thomas Rupert 51
W. 129
Tebbett, A. 129
Alvin 130
J. 81
Mrs 130
Reuben 47, 135
Tebbutt, W. 42
Thomas Danks & Co Ltd, 42
Thompson, F. 123
Thorn, Alfred 45
Thorne, 128
Thorpe, J. 123
Titchener, Mrs 61, 120
Tomlinson, Captain 35, 127
W. 84
Toplis, 32
Toplis, family 127
H. 127, 131
Hilda 127
Hilda Selina 103
L. 127
Leonard 103
Townroe, 32
Townsend, Mr 60, 61
T.A. 61
Turner, C. 84, 92
C.A. 84, 114
Cornelius 55
Lina 55
Mary Ann 55
Warner 39, 90
Turton, Mrs 52

Ullathorne, Thomas 42

Vallance & Blythe, 67
Vallance, see Charles J. Vallance and Sons, 42
Vincent, Arthur 58, 103
Eliza 16
family 17
James 15, 16
Mr 39, 129

Wagstaff, Muriel 93
Wainman, Mr 52

Wakefield, 30, 48, 108, 128
A. 81
F. 48
M 48
Mr 108
Mrs 42, 108
T. 81, 84
Tom 25
Walker, Dorothy 54
E. 84
Mr 60
Mrs 71
Walter, Hobson 50
Ward, A. 95
Mr 60
T. 54
Wardle, J.T. 114
Warner, Councillor 19
Dorothy 60
Warner.- Turner, Mrs 42
Warren, A. 84, 118
Wass, G. 84
O. 118
Watson, James 51
Mr 62
T. 95
Tacey 54
Webb, C. Rev. 33
Webster, Corporal 122
Edward Wall 58
J. 122
John William 58
Weir, Captain 131
Welsh, Norah 93
Westwick, Miss 131
Wharmby, H. 85
Wheatley, Geo. 113
White, 79
J. 84, 118
T. 129
Whiteoak, F. 71
Mr 69
Mrs 61
Whitney, M Miss 42
Whysall, W. 118
W.W. 84
Wilkinson, F.H. 123
William Exley & Sons, 42

Williams,R.H. 55
Willings, Nurse 42
Willis, see Jones & Willis Ltd, 42
Willoughby, 55
Mrs 72
T. 71
Wilson, H. 123
Miss 128
William 7
Winfield, 70
S. 70, 71, 72
Winter, Arthur 58
Gertrude 58
I Miss 42
Withers, J. 81
Wood, J. 136
Mrs 128
Woollens, Norah 36
Woolley, Peter 125
Woolrich, J. 85
Wragg, A. 126
Wright, G. 95
J Rev 53
J. 55
James 15
Mary 15
Mrs 27
Wroe, Arthur 130
Edwin 130

Young, Francis 58
Frank Bevise, 126
Hilda Mary 58, 103